ROYAL YACHTS
OF THE WORLD

4053

ENGINEER

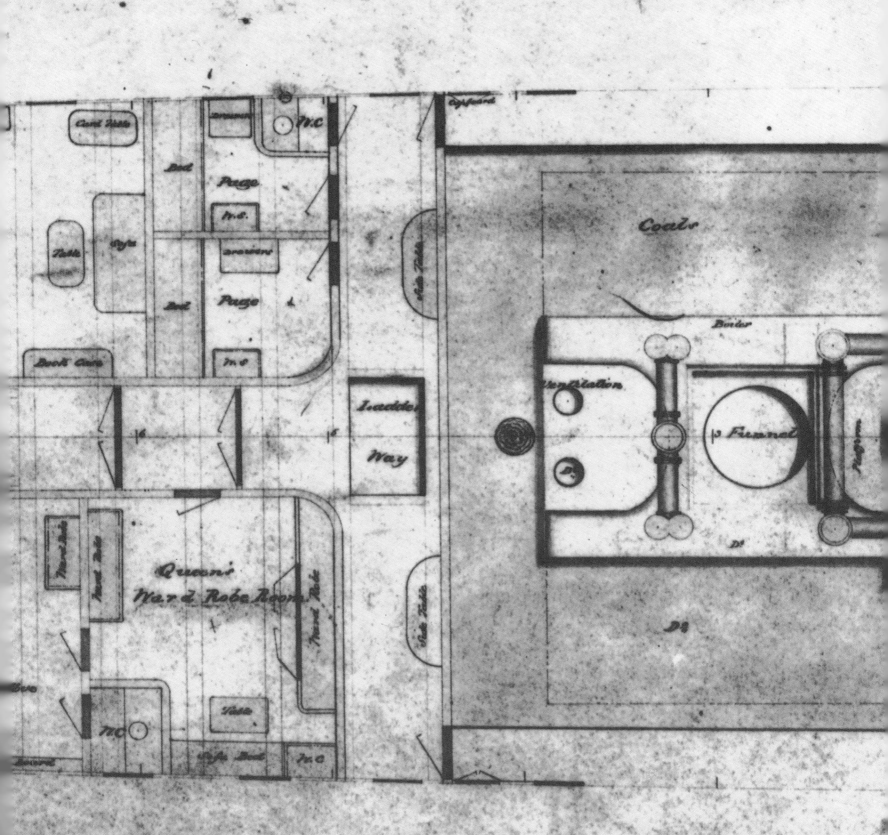

ROYAL YACHTS OF THE WORLD

TIM MADGE

THOMAS REED PUBLICATIONS

A DIVISION OF THE ABR COMPANY LIMITED

Also by Tim Madge

National Newspapers
Media in Britain
Beyond the BBC
Maiden (with Tracy Edwards)
A Ship too Far
Long Voyage Home
The Last Hero

Copyright © Tim Madge 1997 (text)
Copyright © The ABR Company Limited 1997 (compilation)

The right of Tim Madge to be identified as the author of this work has been asserted by him
in accordance with the Copyright, Designs and Patents Act 1988.

Published by
Thomas Reed Publications
(a division of The ABR Company Limited)
19 Bridge Road, Hampton Court,
East Molesey, Surrey KT8 9EU
United Kingdom

First published in Great Britain 1997

A CIP catalogue record for this book is available from the British Library

Editorial direction Laura Ivill
Design and page layout Eric Drewery
Picture research Tony Moore

Colour origination
Primary Colours
Printed in Hong Kong
Midas Printing Limited

ISBN 0 901281 74 3

Registered at Stationers' Hall

Endpapers illustration Detail of Admiralty plans of the *Victoria and Albert II*
Illustration facing title page The *Victoria and Albert II,* Queen Victoria's favourite ship
Title page detail The binnacle and bell of *Britannia*

CONTENTS

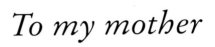
To my mother

ACKNOWLEDGEMENTS

An enormous effort went into producing this book and to ensure that it came out on time. Many people contributed to this but among those I would like to single out for special mention are: David Hodge, Bob Todd and Lindsay Macfarlane at the National Maritime Museum, Greenwich; Frances Diamond of the Royal Archives, Windsor; Malcolm Wood in Antibes for photographs, information and suggestions; Antonia Fleishman for her Greek translations; Ron Valent for his work on Dutch texts; Oliver Madge similarly for his German translations. Bob Marsh helped in numerous ways in dealing with various royal households in Europe. In the United States I would like to thank Raymond Teichman of the Franklin D Roosevelt Library and Randy Sowell of the Harry S Truman Library; thanks, too, to all the other libraries of former presidents of the United States who gave help. In Germany Thomas Weis of the Bibliothek fur Zeitgeschichte provided much useful data; in France I am indebted to the staff of the various maritime museums. Early on, considerable help was provided by the naval attachés of a number of embassies in London. Later in the research I was ably assisted by staff at the library on the *Illustrated London News*, by British Library staff and by those of the London Library. I had important information provided by the Business Records Department of the University of Glasgow and by the Mitchell Library.

Various other libraries and archives in the north of England pointed me in the right direction. Valuable information on the possible replacement for *Britannia* was provided by Maldwin Drummond; similar help on the *Savarona* was given by Steve Howard. Ingram Murray of the new *Shtandart* project found us pictures of the exciting build in St Petersburg. The staff of Beken of Cowes were interrupted in their annual busiest period (Cowes Week) by my inquiries which they handled with aplomb. The staff of the Hulton Getty photolibrary were also of great help, as were those of the Mary Evans Picture Library.

Three people remain to thank, without which this book would simply not have appeared. First, Tony Moore, the picture researcher who came to the project at a critical time and who rapidly made himself indispensable; he has emerged triumphant, as the book testifies. Eric Drewery, the designer, has excelled at producing a sparkling and vibrant record of the ever-changing world of royal yachts from their origins to today, creating a skilful blend of text and images. Finally, my editor, Laura Ivill, who has co-ordinated and overseen the production process as well as managing to overcome an author's reluctance at seeing his text improved immeasurably by a patient application of a blend of tlc and a big stick. My debt to her is lasting.

Tim Madge

CHAPTER 1

SHIPS OF STATE
AN INTRODUCTION

They have been used by emperors and empresses, kings and queens, princes and princesses, presidents and their wives. Some have been the most beautiful ships ever built. All have had an avowed purpose: to represent in physical form the essence of their owners in a way that the bricks, stones and mortar of land-built palaces cannot. For ships move, and it has been the stately progression of these vessels across the seas that has come to symbolise the power and glory of the state. Royalty, too, have found in royal yachts a means to escape from both the intrusive stare of their subjects and the burden of office. Ships provide the opportunity for royalty to leave the cares and woes of everyday life behind – if only for a short time – while allowing real privacy. All this has contributed to their survival, and continues to do so today.

Ships have always exuded power: they are still the largest moving objects created by mankind. Frequently they have been beautiful to look at: it is easy to imagine an ancient Egyptian royal barge floating down the Nile inspiring the toiling serfs on her banks with awe; similarly with the triremes of Greece, and Persian galleys, or the high-sterned and over-decorated galleons of the Spanish silver fleet.

These ships of state were utilitarian. We see a revolution in the idea of royal yachts with King Charles II and his love of small yachts. He introduced to a wider audience the idea of cruising and racing small, fast ships – originally from Holland – for pleasure. This came about when he finally fled England in 1651, eventually to end up in Holland, and we can imagine the daily frustrations he faced. Kicking his heels among the flat plains and inland waterways, strolling along the dykes of the Netherlands, his amusements would have been few. The attractions of hunting and

Detail above Subtle but strong: the bows of *Britannia*.

Right The power and the glory of the monarchy as symbolised by the 1824 figurehead from the *Royal Charlotte*.

Below Charles II, the King who brought fun to royal sailing.

fishing across this landscape, or just pottering about in boats, were quite probably the only course open to him to prevent his lively mind from sinking into despair. If one thing is certain it's that the Dutch would have been delighted to hand on to him their consummate skills in the handling of the myriad small craft that populated their daily life.

The Dutch used small boats the way the rest of Europe used horses. For nine long years the English King had leisure enough to learn what Samuel Pepys would later call 'the skills of the common seaman'. Charles would have learned something priceless here: the skills of small sail-boat handling, so different from that of big ship handling. Freed from the daily cares of running a country, he discovered too the pleasure of setting one against another in races.

On his triumphant return to England in 1660, King Charles seems to have had little time for revenge, much more for the urgent business of enjoying life. Part of that enjoyment was racing the Dutch *jacht*, that the burghers of Amsterdam had given to him as a present, and later racing modified versions of this sailing ship, built in English yards. In an instant, on the wings of the Restoration, the English found in their midst the world's first small royal racing yachts. The awe that had been inspired in Egyptian peasant farmers as much as 4,000 years before, was replaced in the casual onlooker by glee as two or more yachts swooped and plunged on the waters of the Thames, tacking back and forth across the wide estuarine waters down towards the sea and back again. This

Below Vice-regal barge from a Thebes' wall painting c. 1360BC.

was the seed planted by the Merry Monarch – it would take 200 years before it flowered fully.

Meanwhile, the English kings had had their appetites whetted for this kind of conveyance, not just for pleasure alone, but also as the means by which their dignity could be preserved whenever they had to travel. Although he loved to race yachts, Charles II is said to have loved cruising in them even more.

There is reasoning here, never explicit in documents until well into the nineteenth century, in which the royal yacht becomes the means by which royal persons are able to travel sedately yet efficiently, while retaining a high degree of privacy and that indefinable dignity of office. The traditional means by which this was accomplished, on horseback or by carriage, lacked finesse, although these still had to be used on shorter trips. Jumping ahead, the newer means, by train, although efficient, had something less desirable to offer, by way of the motion and the commotion of smoke and noise. Crucially, it lacked dignity: the royal train might well have been immediately preceded through the welcoming town or city by a cattle train – or worse.

From the innocent early days of the royal yacht the purely pleasurable elements began to be down-played. The utilitarian purpose, heavily laden with the ceremonial, began to exert more and more influence. After the reign of William III (1688-1702) the somewhat dour Hanoverians lighted on their royal yachts much more as ornate transport than as

Above The *Cleveland,* built in 1671 for Charles II, from a painting by Willem Van de Velde the Younger.

sailing yachts. And so it would remain across Europe and beyond for years to come.

From what we know in the rest of the world at that time, outside Europe, royal progress on water was generally limited to rivers and coastal traffic, for whatever purpose, where the ornately decorated royal barge came to its own localised formal fruition. But it was to be Europe and European norms that would grow to dominance through the eighteenth century. In matters maritime, as the fortunes of the Spanish and Portuguese waned, the conflicts between the English, the Dutch and the French would be those that counted, although to the north of Europe the Swedes would continue their long-standing series of clashes with a largely still-slumbering Russia. The French monarchy, alone of all these powers, seems to have been less bothered by the need for any kind of dedicated royal ship, yacht or otherwise, than the rest. In the seventeenth century Louis XIV, the Sun King, had created an extraordinary spectacle at Versailles of a miniature ocean with miniature ships sailing on it; for him this was, apparently, enough.

The German-born English Kings needed to travel frequently across the Channel back to their beloved Hanover. As time went by, they found it pleasurable to anchor one or more of these by-now much larger yachts off a port on the south coast, notably Brighton and Weymouth, thereby inventing, as royalty often did, a new fashion – in this case for the seaside and all its attractions.

This was the prelude to the whole notion of sailing yachts for pleasure. If the English (by the nineteenth century the *British*) royal family led the stampede, it was merely because Britain was turning itself almost daily into the world's first industrialised nation. However, the Dutch royal family, appropriately, owned the world's first steam yacht, but the British were not far behind and, as befitted a modern go-ahead nation, jumped aboard this kind of ship with a mighty enthusiasm. The Victorian steam yacht captured the imagination of the regal world. It became the potent symbol of power, modernity, dignity and opulence. Because of the technology involved, along with a desire to give the royals of the time the very best, these ships were often among the fastest afloat, creating a further reinforcement of the feelings among their subjects that their rulers had the right to be who they were.

As we shall see, the Victorian age also found time to re-invent yacht racing, a sport that attracted the Prince of Wales. Thus, after 200 years, the term 'royal yacht' returned, in part, to mean what King Charles II would have taken it to be. At the same time, the Victorian steam yacht, with or without auxiliary sails, swept across the world, attracting royalty wherever it entered port. The British dominated the field as builders for a long while, culminating in the moment when, at the turn of the century, one man, GL Watson, was the fashion guru to whom everyone turned for designs of both classic steam yachts and classic racing yachts.

Below On a state visit to the Pacific island of Tuvalu, the Queen and the Duke of Edinburgh are carried out of the sea on ceremonial canoe barges on which they have disembarked from the royal yacht *Britannia*.

By then, though, things were beginning to sour a little, notably with the royal yacht equivalent of an arms race. This was not just between the British and the Germans. Even the aging Queen Victoria was discomforted, not so much by her German relations and their pretensions but by her British advisers who, against her ardent desire, insisted she had a new yacht to replace her beloved *Victoria and Albert II*, the vanguard of its kind. Mercifully, she never had to swap her old and faithful yacht for the new one, which she loathed heartily. By the time she died in 1901, royal yachts were becoming huge ships: the *Standart* for the Russians, the *Hohenzollern* for the Germans, the *Trinacria* for the Italians, and the third *Victoria and Albert*. Some idea of where this was going is provided by the planned replacement for the *Hohenzollern* – easily as big as a transatlantic liner, although it was never completed.

The aftermath of the First World War waved goodbye to all this, as it did to many of the royal families of Europe. In the interlude between the two world wars, royalty lost much of its former opulence to the twentieth century's growing obsession for efficiency – and for democracy. It was no longer thought to be politic to have such large vessels sailing back and forth for the pleasure of their owners. The pomp and circumstance argument had been drowned in the mud of Flanders, and if royal advisers wanted an awful example of where disregard for these issues led, they only had to turn to Russia, by then the Soviet Union, and the fate of the Tsar and his family.

By the 1930s, though, some of the world's republics had lighted upon state yachts for the same reasons royalty had used them. Some, like Kemal Ataturk's dictatorship in newly westernising Turkey, inherited a long line of royal yachts but chose to buy abroad. Others, notably the United States, with its strong democratic credentials, hung somewhere in the middle. Early United States official yachts had been lent from the US Navy or borrowed from rich citizens such as the Astors. When official yachts were commissioned they were small, motor riverboats rather than ocean-going ships, and presidents were forced to use the larger ships of the Navy, such as the *USS Indianapolis,* when they needed something larger. This fitted the mood. In Europe, too, small was becoming beautiful, a feeling reinforced by the outcome of the Second World War.

Grateful for the King's efforts on their behalf, the recently liberated Norwegian people spent £250,000 of their own money to

Below A carved scene from the Temple of Horus at Edfu, showing the god in a boat spearing a hippo who represents the god Seth, a rival for the crown of Egypt.

buy him a medium-sized yacht, the old *Philante*, as a coming-home present. The Dutch royal family went back to their pre-war riverboat *De Piet Hein*. It was the British who broke away from this downsizing when they built the royal yacht *Britannia* in the early 1950s. She had been on the drawing board since the mid 1930s when it was felt the third *Victoria and Albert* needed to be replaced, but the war intervened.

The accession of the young Queen Elizabeth in 1953 had brought a new mood of optimism across the country after the long years of economic trouble which followed 1945. As much as anything, building the new royal yacht fitted into a hope, rather than a promise, that the future would be rosy. The British people found it hard to grasp the uncomfortable fact that although they had been on the winning side in the war, they had not won it. The nation had bankrupted itself hanging on, until the Americans and the Soviet Union stepped in. The significance was missed at the time but while the British were building *Britannia*, President Eisenhower, as head of state of the world's most powerful nation, had the use of a few very modest motor cruisers.

The 1950s saw the end of another raft of royal yachts: those belonging to most of the remaining royal families outside the Gulf, such as the Egyptians and Iraqis. One, however, survived, and she remains the oldest royal yacht still afloat. Built on the Thames in 1866 and first named *Mahroussa*, she is now called *El Horriya*. In 1997 she is still occasionally used as the Egyptian presidential yacht.

But it has been in the Middle East, with its soaring revenues from oil, particularly from the 1970s, that there has been a revival in royal yachts as opulent floating palaces. Some are overblown beyond belief for Western tastes, others are more discreet, more stately. That they exist speaks volumes for the survival of a kind of ship that goes back, one way or another, to that earliest of Middle Eastern royal vessels: the funerary barge of the Pharaoh Cheops. The wheel has come full circle 5,000 years on.

Below The *Abdul Aziz,* one of the many Saudi royal yachts, and, until 1997, the world's biggest. The Sultan of Brunei has ordered one larger still.

CHAPTER 2

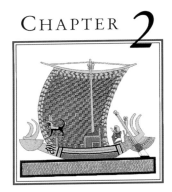

FROM PHARAOHS TO PRINCES

The ship, in one form or another, has always held its audience in awe, none more so than in ancient times. But taking to waters other than slow-flowing rivers or along the coasts of relatively calm seas held immense dangers. Those princes and kings of times long past who ventured out to sea in pursuit of their goals became as one with their ships and gave us some of the most enduring myths we have. From across the world come legends of great sea voyages to colonise the unknown world: the Incas from South America to the islands of the South Pacific; more fantastically the ancient Egyptians from North Africa to South America; and the Chinese, perhaps, from Asia to North America. All these routes have been prospected in recent times to see if the legends could be based in fact. What is not certain is whether these vessels would have had more than just wild seafaring adventurers on board. Plain logic suggests that there would have been strong leaders in charge, and that it's likely these would have been royally connected, given the nature of the times.

In the Mediterranean, that cradle of Western civilisation, much more is known: the voyages of Odysseus; the great sea-faring invasion planned by Agamemnon; the battles between Persians and Greeks; the quests of the Roman Emperors. The ships built and sailed by the royal leaders would have been more highly decorated, carried more sails of greater quality, and crews of higher mettle than the average. Early kings were also warriors and this intertwining of roles would not have been to the detriment of the power and dignity of the 'monarchy'. In later times, however, and most obviously with the great voyages of the Vikings out of their Scandinavian stronghold to the far west of North America, the lead ship would not have been so different from those that followed. We

Detail above Egyptian galley, from a mural.

Above right The sacred boat of Prince Mourhet, from a painting in his tomb at Giza.

Below right A Roman trireme leaving the Arsenal (1st century AD). By this time ships were potent symbols of power.

Above A Viking raiding fleet races across the North Sea (9th-10th centuries).

Left An attack on the English coast. The Vikings were feared for their legendary sailing skills as much as for their warlike culture, both of which helped to create myths of invincibility.

Above A Saxon longship of about 1000AD. Open vessels like these were very seaworthy despite their size, and they would make many passages in open seas.

have an account of what a royal Viking ship looked like, when, in the tenth century, King Harold of Norway gave King Athelstan of West Saxons and Mercians a ship whose bow was wrought in gold, with sails of purple canvas. These longships of the time are those most associated with the Viking raiders terrorising the coasts of southern Europe, as well as the British Isles. The royal versions were much more highly decorated, usually with figures of men, birds and other animals. They were galleys – propelled by oars as well as by a single sail, and steered by oars on either side of the quarter, at the stern.

In 1040 Earl Godwin presented one of these ships to King Hardicanute. A description says it was 'sumptuously gilded and rowed by eighty men, each of whom wore on his arm a bracelet of gold weighing sixteen ounces'. This ship, too, had purple sails, a colour associated with royalty for centuries. This custom of royal ships having purple sails continued throughout the Middle Ages – one of the last known about was the ship of Henry V of England (1413-1422) when he sailed from England to France under a purple sail embroidered in gold with the coats of arms of the two countries.

In 973 the English King Edgar was rowed down the River Dee by eight lesser kings in his royal barge from Chester to the monastery of St John the Baptist and back. 'No fleet,' says an account of the time, 'was so daring, nor army so strong.'

Until William the Conqueror (1066-1087) there seems to have been no

distinction, in English history at least, between kings' ships and what, in modern parlance, we would call naval ships. William the Conqueror led the invasion of Britain in his own ship, the *Mora,* said to have been the gift of Queen Mathilda. In the Bayeux Tapestry the *Mora* is bigger than the other ships, her prow decorated with a lion's head.

Ships by and large were still deemed to be the king's property. He ordered their movements and sailed on them whenever he pleased. But one, particularly, was kept apart. This type of vessel was called *esnecca* or *snekkja,* words from Scandinavia meaning a long, fast galley. These were, in effect, the royal yachts of their time. During all of this period, up to the late Middle Ages, English kings held extensive lands in France and there was a need for a regular and fast service across the Channel.

One of these ships was wrecked on the coast of Normandy in 1120. As the story goes, Henry II, then in France, had decided to return to England. At Barfleur his ships were gathered – the finest being *La Blanche Nef,* a galley of 50 oars commanded by Thomas Fitz-Stephen. Henry asked Fitz-Stephen to take Prince William, then 17 and his only legitimate son and heir, on this ship. William left on *La Blanche Nef* along with a number of young noblemen and women, but by the time she sailed, the king had already gone. Sadly, the crew of *La Blanche Nef* had been drinking heavily, and, hoping they might catch up with the King's ship, pulled too carelessly along the coast and struck a rock. Only one sailor survived. The King is said never to have smiled again.

Left Ships fit for capturing a kingdom: William the Conqueror's own vessel, the *Mora,* is seen in the centre with her lion-headed prow.

An *esnecca* is known to have been in use in 1166 when Henry II sailed from Portsmouth to Normandy, and in 1174 and 1176 when his daughter also went across to France. At this time the *esnecca* was usually kept in readiness at one of the Cinque Ports.

King Richard the Lionheart (1189-1199) assembled a fleet for the crusade he led, sailing in his own *Trench le Mer.* He was on board during the battle off Acre (on the coast of modern Syria) against the Saracens. When he was released from captivity by the Emperor Henry VI of France, he sent to England for the commander of this same ship and embarked on her from Antwerp in 1194. Some details are known from this period about this vessel – for instance that the King's cabin was panelled. In 1210 the master of the king's galley is mentioned as being a Richard of London.

By the end of the thirteenth century galleys had been replaced by a type of ship called a cog, a full sailing ship, probably rather short in length but of a very broad beam. Sir Nicholas Nicolas in his *History of the Royal Navy* says: 'the king's own ships, the *Thomas* and the *Christopher* – the latter the most celebrated ship for her size and beauty – were "cogs"... a first class vessel of the fourteenth century'. They were of about 200 tons burden (that is, they would have been able to carry about 200 tons cargo). The *Thomas* was sunk while King Edward I was on board, at the Battle of Les Espagnols sur Mer. Other ships of this time that had royal connections were the *Swallow,* described as a 'fluve'

Below A 14th-century miniature showing the Knights of the Holy Ghost embarking for a Crusade in about 1100.

Left A ship from about 1300 displaying the royal arms on her sail.

(a large, flat ship, usually to be seen inland), the galley *La Philippa*, and the *Grace de Dieu*. *La Philippa* had a single mast and yard, a bowsprit and a red sail. She was rowed with 80 oars. In *Grace de Dieu* King Edward III cruised along the coast of Normandy and Britanny in 1372.

As well as sea-going vessels, there were royal barges. In 1400, the year of the death of Richard II, one of these was painted red and adorned with collars and garters of gold, each collar containing a fleur-de-lis, each garter a leopard.

By the time of Henry V (1413-1422) we know that the royal ships were seen as the personal possession of the monarch because the first orders in council made by him directed the sale of his ships to pay off the debts of his predecessor. Gilded barges on the Thames are heard of again during the time of the Tudors, and at this time the royal ships were getting both larger and more ornate. When Henry VIII went to Boulogne in 1520 he is depicted standing on the deck of his royal ship which has cloth-of-gold sails.

The Tudor period was one of great turmoil, and English kings and queens, having lost the last of their lands in France, didn't care to venture far offshore. Queen Elizabeth I (1558-1603), despite her long association with some of the greatest sailors the world has ever produced – Drake, Raleigh, Howard of Effingham – only ever embarked on the placid waters of the Thames in her royal barge, and then not often.

Below Richard II aboard his royal barge at Rotherhithe in 1381.

The reign of James I (1603-1625) changed all that, albeit in a small way to begin with. In 1604 Phineas Pett, a member of a well-known ship-building family, had orders from the Lord High Admiral to build as fast as he could a miniature ship for Prince Henry, the King's eldest son. Prince Henry was to name this ship the *Disdain*. Phineas Pett left an account of this commission: 'About January 15th, 1604, a letter was sent post-haste to Chatham from my Honourable Lord High Admiral Howard, commanding me with all possible speed to build a little vessel for the young Prince Henry to disport himself in about London bridge, and acquaint his Grace with shipping, and the manner of that element; setting me down the proportions and the manner of garnishing, which was to be like the work of the *Ark Royal*, battlementwise. This little ship was in length 25 feet by the keel, and in breadth 12 feet, garnished with painting and carving, both within board and without, very curiously, according to his Lordship's directions.'

Pett worked day and night by torch and candlelight, and the ship was launched on 6th March 'with a noise of drums, trumpets, and such like ceremonies'. Pett was attached to the Court of King James as keeper and Captain of this tiny royal ship which, he says: 'was manned with almost all boatswains of the Navy, and other choice men', and which was then sailed from Chatham to the Thames where she arrived on

Above The *Ark Royal*, which was also known as the *Anne Royal*, on which the *Disdain* is said to be based.

Right inset Prince Henry, proud owner of the *Disdain* and the eldest son of James I, from a miniature by Isaac Oliver.

Right The embarkation of the Elector of Hanover at Dover on 25th April 1613, from a painting by Adam Willaerts. The smaller *Disdain* is shown on the far right of the picture.

22nd March, and anchored off Blackwall. She was then moved from there to moor by the Tower of London where she was visited by Prince Henry and by the Lord High Admiral who was delighted by what he saw. After that she was moved further up the river again to anchor off the Palace Whitehall.

A few days later the Prince came on board again with others of the royal household. The ship weighed anchor, dropped down the river, 'and then his Grace, according to the manner in such cases, with a great bowle of wine, christened the ship and called her by the name of the *Disdain*'.

In 1608 Pett, with Prince Henry, then 14, visited Woolwich where they could see the *Prince Royal* being built. King James gave the young heir to the throne this great ship, but the Prince never got to sail in her as he died in 1612. The *Disdain* largely disappears from view after this, although she is on the Navy List of 1618 where she was rated at 30 tons burden.

With the *Disdain* a turning point is reached in the story of royal yachts, at least as regards Europe. Although she was built for a child, ostensibly to help Prince Henry to learn about ships, she was for pleasure too. This change of emphasis was written into the plans for the *Disdain*; a seed was sown. It would take another Stuart monarch, forced into exile, to discover anew just how much fun sailing a small craft could be.

CHAPTER 3

ROYAL SHIPS TO ROYAL YACHTS

It is to the Dutch, strictly speaking, that we owe the word yacht. And it is to King Charles II that we owe a greater and lasting debt for having introduced both cruising yachts and yacht racing to England. For hundreds of years the Dutch had used boats the way the rest of Europe used horses, and the yacht, or *jacht*, is thought to have derived from *ter jacht gaen* – to go hunting. These small, fast ships had also accompanied Dutch fighting ships to sea for many years, acting as advice boats to the fleet.

When King Charles II fled finally to Holland in 1651 after the triumph of the Parliamentarians in the English Revolution (1643-1660), he had many years of enforced leisure in which to study the ways of the Dutch, no doubt learning much of his later proclaimed and attested seamanship from them. But Charles was no stranger to sailing. After the Battle of Naseby in 1645, he had fled via the Scilly Isles to the Channel Islands, steering the ship which took him, the *Proud Black Eagle,* for some of the way. While he stayed in the Channel Islands he kept himself busy sailing – a small sailing vessel was sent over from St Malo for him.

In Holland, after 1651, Charles would have come across a multitude of different sailing vessels, many very different from those he would have been used to seeing on the other side of the Channel. *Jachts* were not a type of vessel as such – the Dutch used the word to describe a class of small, fast sailing ships. They also raced them, much as the English raced horses.

Detail above Charles II, father of sailing yachts for pleasure and the first king in Europe to own a royal yacht.

Right A model of the yacht *Mary,* the first of Charles II's yachts. She was a gift from the burghers of Amsterdam in 1660.

At the Restoration of the English monarchy in 1660, Charles II started his journey homeward along the coast of Holland in a *jacht,* which had previously been owned by his late brother-in-law, the Prince of Orange. The King boarded his *jacht* at Breda, and it had been intended there should be a dinner on board, but the wind was so strong and the waves so fierce that Mary, the Princess Royal, had to lie down while the fleet sailed for Rotterdam. Here the King left his *jacht,* travelled overland to Scheveningen, where he embarked on one of the English ships waiting offshore, the *Naseby.* Samuel Pepys, the diarist, who was on board, noted that this ship changed her name the very moment the King came aboard her – to the *Royal Charles.*

It was because the King was so pleased with this *jacht* that the burgomaster of Amsterdam begged to be allowed to present him with one of the same style. The merchants sent over a similar vessel which arrived in the Thames two months after the King's return. He named her the *Mary* after his sister the Princess Royal, who had also sailed back in her, and who was the mother of the future William III.

It is the *Mary* from which it may be fairly said all modern yachts owe their inheritance. Originally built for the Dutch East India Company she was 52 feet long, had a beam of 18-and-half feet, and drew only three feet. She was fitted, like all Dutch *jacht*s, with leeboards, and had a crew of 30. In today's terms she would have looked not dissimilar to a Thames barge. Her figurehead was a unicorn, and the royal arms were emblazoned on her stern. Her high coach-roof and the side windows of the stern cabin were ornately carved. The interiors of the cabins were decorated and gilded, and some of the best artists of the period had been engaged to produce beautiful paintings and sculptures to put in them. Eight ornamental cannon projected from her gunports, decorated with gilded wreaths. Sadly, she was wrecked on the Skerrys, near Holyhead, in 1675; her wreck was discovered by divers in 1970. A model of the *Mary* is in the National Maritime Museum, London, where she can be admired for what she was – a very pretty little ship indeed.

Pepys remained intrigued by the little foreign ships that Charles had fallen in love with, and makes a number of entries about both them and the King's great love of racing them on the Thames, for after the *Mary* there came a whole succession. Charles managed to own 27 in all. The Master Shipwright of the Woolwich Dockyard, Sir Anthony Deane, told Pepys that 'in the year '60 the Dutch gave His Majesty a yacht called the *Mary,* whence came the improvement of our present yachts, for until that time we had not heard such a name in England'. Pepys also noted that 'to the office, and after dinner by water to White Hall, where I found the King gone this morning by five of the clock to see a Dutch pleasure-boat below bridge, where he dines, and my Lord with him. The king do tire all his people that are about him with early rising since he come'. In November Pepys went on board the *Mary,* noting it was

Below Samuel Pepys, the diarist, who was fascinated by his monarch's ability as a 'common sailor'.

Above A group of early royal yachts off Greenwich in the River Thames. King Charles II had 27 in all.

Right Pencil drawing of the *Katherine,* a royal yacht of 1661, and only the fourth in a long line.

one of the finest objects he had ever seen. He was with Commissioner Pett who was there to measure the ship and to make notes for a similar vessel the King had ordered. This was to be the *Katherine*, a royal yacht of 90 tons, built for £1,335 at Deptford. She was named for the King's future wife, Katherine of Braganza, Infanta of Portugal, whom he married at Portsmouth on 22nd May 1662. The *Katherine* was a close copy of the *Mary*, except for her greater seven-foot draught. Later she was joined by the *Anne*, of 94 tons, named for the Duchess of York.

The Dutch *jachts* had been typical of many sailing ships in Holland: broad of beam and with a shallow draught, perfect for the constantly silting-up Dutch waterways. The leeboards were to improve their

Above The *Royal Escape* – the coastal brig in which Charles finally escaped from England in 1651, posing as a penurious merchant.

sailing to windward. The English shipwrights, who now had a chance to study this design, set about improving on it for the very different sailing conditions around the British Isles. Between 1661 and 1663 Peter and Christopher Pett and Thomas Shish designed five royal yachts in all, based on a melding of the *jacht* with contemporary English warship patterns. The others were the *Jemmy*, the *Charles* and the *Henrietta*.

The *Katherine* continued in service until she was captured by the Dutch in 1673 (this being the time of the Dutch Wars). She was back the following year, but meanwhile a new *Katherine* had been laid down. In fact, the name stayed with one royal yacht or another all through the rest of the seventeenth and then the eighteenth centuries.

The *Anne* was sold in 1686 to be used by the London Customs House. The *Bezan*, 35 tons, 34 feet long and with a three-foot six-inch draught, came over from Holland in 1661. Although *bezan* means mizen in Dutch, she was a single-masted gaff-rigged cutter. She had the reputation of being a very fast sailer indeed.

It was in racing these ships that Charles II took great pleasure. The diarist Evelyn records that in a race between the *Katherine* and the *Anne*, from Greenwich to Gravesend and back, the King lost to the Duke of York. They were accompanied by a kitchen boat, providing all the lunches, suppers and other meals for the royal party. As time went by the problem of all the catering was solved by building a royal yacht specifically for that purpose: her name, of course, was *Kitchen*.

Above The Royal yacht *Saudadoes*, known as Queen Katherine's Little Ship, 1688. Her name means 'intense longing' in Portuguese.

Inset Katherine of Braganza, the long-suffering wife of Charles II.

Three of the many royal yachts of the reign of Charles II are worthy of note. The first was the *Royal Escape* in which Charles had left England for Holland in 1651. After the decisive Battle of Worcester on 3rd September, Charles had had plenty of adventures, including the famous sojourn in an oak tree. He had travelled by way of Bristol, down to the Dorset coast, back through Wiltshire and Hampshire and then again to the coast of Sussex. At the George Inn in Brighton he met the Captain of the ship that was to take him to France – at that time she was called the *Surprise* – a suitable enough name, as her Captain, Nicholas Tattersall, was the only person who knew the identity of her illustrious passengers. The crew were told the royal party were merchants fleeing creditors. The coastal brig made her run across the Channel, and they landed at Fécamp.

Charles retained enormous affection for this brig, and when he came back to England 11 years later he bought her from her Captain, and renamed her *Royal Escape*. For many years she was moored off Whitehall where the King would show her off to other royalty. In the Navy List of the time, she was called a smack of 34 tons, 30 feet long, with a beam of 14-and-a-half feet, drawing seven feet.

For his Queen the King ordered a yacht to be built which Katherine named the *Saudadoes*. She was used for excursions on the River Thames. Her Portuguese name is hard to translate, the plural meaning 'good luck' or 'good wishes'; the nuance however is 'intense longing'

Left One of the Pett brothers, famous for their adaptation of the Dutch *jachts* to suit King Charles II's tastes and the very different English conditions. From a painting by Sir Pieter Lely.

Below The Duchess of Portsmouth whose nickname was 'Fubbs' and after whom a royal yacht was named.

and one can only speculate what longing the Queen might have had in mind: for Charles to stop his dalliances, or for her homeland, perhaps? The *Saudadoes* was sent to Portugal twice for the Queen to hear news of her country. In the Pepysian Library in Magdalene College, Cambridge, an account by her Captain, James Jenifer, of one of these voyages provides information on the state of affairs that existed in Portugal in 1672-3, plus sketches and diagrams. The *Saudadoes* was rebuilt in 1674 as a sixth-rater, of 188 tons, mounting 16 guns.

If part of the Queen's intense longing was over her husband's infidelities, she could hardly have been pleased when the King later had the *Fubbs* built. This was the King's nickname for the Duchess of Portsmouth, with whom he was notoriously involved. It means plump or chubby, a female form much in favour at the time, as witnessed by Rubens' great portraits.

The *Fubbs* was ketch-rigged, a form King Charles claimed he had invented. Built by Phineas Pett at Greenwich in 1682, she had a length overall of 80 feet, a beam of 21 feet and drew just under 10 feet. Her tonnage was 148. She was exceptionally fast, not least because of her very tall mainmast. She carried square topsails with loose-footed fore and aft sails; the mizen sail had a long lateen yard which later became the gaff of a leg-of-mutton-shaped sail.

The royal cabin aft was entered from a richly decorated ante-room and was panelled in carved oak with an inlaid floor. It included a four-poster bed covered with silk and brocade. An account by the Reverend John Gostling of a voyage on her around the Kent coast remarked that all had been going well, with much singing (of which the King was very fond), when the wind began to rise. 'The king and the Duke of York were necessitated, in order to preserve the vessel, to handle the sails like common seamen; but by good providence they escaped to land.' The *Fubbs* was rebuilt in 1701, 1729 and 1749, and broken up in 1781.

King Charles' seamanship was legendary. According to Pepys 'he possessed a transcendent mastery of all maritime knowledge, and two leagues travel at sea was more pleasure to him than twenty by land'. He also attended many of the launchings of his ships and of the Navy's.

Above James II, with a royal yacht in the background, from a portrait by Henri Gascard. He had little of his late brother's interest in royal yachts – except as a means of escape from England when he fled in 1688.

On his death it may be fairly said that royal yacht racing died too; it was not to be properly revived for nigh on 200 years. In the meantime, the concept of a royal yacht moved closer to that of a floating palace, as much as that could be engineered within the ships of the day.

The death of King Charles II in 1685 marked a turning point in English history. He left a nation of unprecedented prosperity and social tranquillity. The Merry Monarch was succeeded by his brother James II who in three years, in what now looks like an obscure religious dispute, managed, in effect, to get himself banished. His only recorded use of royal yachts was to send two of them down the river in preparation for his escape. 'Order the *Isabella* and *Anne* yachts to fall down to Erith tomorrow,' he wrote. On his way to France one of his last acts after his abdication was to throw the Great Seal of England into the Thames; it has never been recovered.

The reign of William III (1689-1702) was a happier time altogether. The King, being the Dutch Prince of Orange, had much reason to travel between his new kingdom and his old. At the time of his accession there were eight yachts on the Navy List, including the *Kitchen* and the *Fubbs*. The *Mary* brought Queen Mary over from Holland to Greenwich in February 1689. William and Mary's principal yacht was built for them at Chatham in 1694. The *William and Mary* cost just over £2,000, and was of 152 tons. The King made a number of journeys to Holland in her. She was rebuilt at Deptford in 1765 and continued, with various refits, until 1801. (Six years later a second *William and Mary* was built, lasting until 1847.)

Queen Anne (1702-1714), the last of the Stuarts, did not use her royal yachts very much. One significant build of her reign was the *Charlot,* of 155 tons. This yacht was afterwards rigged as a ketch. She was renamed the *Augusta* in 1761, and was one of the fleet that brought Queen Charlotte to England for her marriage to King George III.

Above Peter the Great, Tsar of Russia, studying shipbuilding at Deptford in 1698.

While the English were busy in the seventeenth century building the foundations of their maritime future, the French were establishing themselves as the European centre for culture through the efforts of *Le Roi Soleil*, King Louis XIV. At Versailles, a great palace was created – his most enduring and magnificent monument – but he didn't stop there. Part of the huge grounds surrounding his masterpiece was turned over to Le Grand Canal, a lake nearly a mile long and nearly 400 feet wide. It was flanked with formal gardens, pavilions, fountains, flights of steps and walkways with vantage points. On it there floated an armada of vessels for the entertainment of King and court. These *chaloupes* and *galiotes* were, in 1679, supplemented with *gondoles* sent from Venice, complete with their *gondoliers*. King Charles II sent to Versailles – she sailed across the Channel – a model, probably half actual size, of an English royal yacht to add to King Louis' collection. In all the excitement Charles forgot to pay his English shipwrights for this extravagant gift. But whatever the outcome of that dispute, several more were built and sent over. The French called them *yaks*.

All these ships did indeed create impressive spectacles for the amusement of the French court. There were manoeuvres and mock battles – costly exercises in regal vanity probably never to be surpassed.

If the French were self-indulgent in their marine antics at court, another European monarch had an altogether different purpose in building what amounted to his first and only royal yacht. Peter the Great, that colossus of Russian imperial history and the man to which late twentieth-century Russia looks to again for inspiration, came to England as part of his search for the means to drag the old primitive

Russia into a post-Mediaeval age. He came solely to learn about shipbuilding. He had already tapped into the knowledge of those other great seventeenth-century shipbuilders, the Dutch. A giant of a man for his time, standing at well over six feet, he must have cut an exotic figure around the east-London dockyards of Deptford, where he was lodging.

As a result of his personal researches, punctuated, if the stories are true, by wild drinking sessions at the local inns, he had the *Standart* designed and built. It was a frigate which became the base on which the imperial Russian Navy was founded. Launched in 1703, she had the Tsar as her first captain, and she remained his favourite ship, closely resembling the English ships of her day. When she was finally laid up, Peter the Great gave orders that she should be kept in St Petersburg as a permanent monument to the art of Russian shipbuilding. Sadly, nothing was done to prevent her rotting away. After his death Catherine the Great gave orders that the *Standart* was to be rebuilt, but nothing was ever done.

Over 200 years later, in 1997, the *Standart* is at last being rebuilt in St Petersburg by a team of volunteers. As this book is published, plans are afoot to sail this magnificent reconstruction back to Britain in 1998, on the 300th anniversary of Peter the Great's visit to England. She will be used as a sail-training ship. In a poetic echo of history, her new builder Victor Martous, travelled to the National Maritime Museum in London to study three models of the time, thought to be exactly like those Peter the Great took home with him. In St Petersburg the project has a stalwart manager in Greg Palmer, a historian from Britain. Thus do

Top A model of a ship that closely resembles the first *Standart*.

Above The reconstruction of the *Standart* underway in St Petersburg in 1996. She is planned to be ready for the 300th anniversary of Peter the Great's visit to Holland and England.

the strands of history sometimes recombine and weave again the past in the present.

Denmark, small in area, but with a mighty seafaring tradition (particularly with the Vikings), had only one royal yacht built in the late seventeenth century, by an English shipwright. The *Elephanten* was laid down in Copenhagen in 1687 by Francis Sheldon working for King Christian I. Rigged as a snow (rather like a small brig), she was just over 90 feet long, had a beam of 23 feet and a draught of nine feet. The snow rig was not dissimilar to the ketch of the time, with a fore and aft mizen and yards on her bowsprit. She carried 18 six-pounders on her main deck and six four-pounders on her quarter deck. In 1690 she was replaced, as the royal yacht, by a much larger ship, the *Cronen*. The *Elephanten*, meanwhile, was used by the Danish Navy until she was wrecked in 1721.

The Swedish monarchs had been troubled for centuries by Russia, their huge neighbour to the east. In the eighteenth century Sweden held parts of modern Finland and all of Norway, and was a powerful Baltic state. In 1778 Gustav III ordered a royal vessel from the English shipwright Frederick Chapman. He had been one of a number of English shipbuilders working in Sweden, and he had been noted for a design of a shallow draught frigate much in use by the navy. The *Amphion* was around 160 feet in length with oars as well as sails. She was brigantine rigged, and she was used by the King for pleasure cruises in and around the myriad islands of the Finnish archipelago. During the Russian War of 1788-90 she served as the royal headquarters. The *Amphion* was finally broken up in 1885.

In 1714, with the reign of Queen Anne at an end, and the English legally united with the Scots, Britain chose to turn away from the turbulent possibilities of a regal succession through the line of King James II. The country looked instead to a small protestant state in Germany, Hanover, for their next king. For over a hundred years the Hanoverians would rule a burgeoning British state. They would see the collapse of one nascent British empire in the loss of the American colonies, and the destruction of Napoleonic France, but would set the course, did they but know it, for Britain to become truly great in the nineteenth century.

As Kings with interests on the continent, to which each returned, and with relatives scattered there, too, it is no surprise that the Hanoverians' use of royal yachts was extensive. George I (1714-1727) had use of as many as 15, and crossed to England in the *Peregrine* in 1714. She was rebuilt two years later, renamed the *Carolina*, then rebuilt again and renamed the *Royal Caroline* in 1733. In his time George I returned six times to Hanover. On the return journey in January 1726, it is recorded that he

Above The Hanoverian royal yacht *Royal Caroline* amidst other vessels off the coast, from a painting of the School of John Clevely the Elder.

Left King George II, from a mezzotint by I. Smith (the original by Godfrey Kneller).

landed at Rye on the Kent coast, having been kept at sea for three days by a violent storm. The following year, during a coach journey taking him back to Hanover once more, he died.

George II (1727-1760) used his yachts for a similar purpose. In 1729 he crossed to Europe in the *Carolina* remaining abroad for the whole summer, and returning in the *William and Mary*. In 1734 the Princess Royal, George II's daughter, was married to the Prince of Orange. After the ceremony in London she travelled to Holland with the Prince in the *Fubbs*. They embarked from Greenwich, but the wind was against them, and they returned to shore to stay with a Dr Holker. The following day they dined on the deck of the *Fubbs*, much to the delight of a large crowd who had gathered to watch.

The Hanoverian period introduced some new royal yachts, but many more were rebuilds and, as we have noted, there were a number of renamings. Thus the second *Charlot*, built in 1710, was renamed the *Augusta* in 1761. She had an overall length of 79 feet, a beam of 22 feet

six inches, and a draught of nine feet six inches. The second *Katherine* was rebuilt at Deptford in 1720, fitted as a ketch in 1736, and finally sold in 1801. The old *Fubbs* lasted until 1729, when she was rebuilt, and then she carried on until 'taken to pieces' in 1781, a hundred years old. A later *Royal Caroline* was renamed *Royal Charlotte* in 1761. She, too, was taken to pieces, in 1820.

The long reign of George III began in 1760 lasting 60 years. He had six yachts at his disposal, the largest being the *Royal Caroline* (later *Royal Charlotte*). The older ones were the *William and Mary*, the *Mary*, the *Katherine*, the *Augusta* and the *Fubbs*. He had only one new yacht built in the first 40 years of his reign – the *Princess Augusta* – to replace the old *Augusta*.

The *Royal Charlotte* was so named because Princess Charlotte of the German principality of Mecklenburg-Strelitz was to be the King's bride. She was brought over in this ship in company with the royal yachts *Mary*, *Katherine*, *Augusta* and *Fubbs* from Stade to Harwich, enduring a severe gale on the way. Royal yachts were also used by George III for naval reviews. In particular, during the long French revolutionary and

Above George III reviews the fleet at Spithead in 1778, from a painting by Dominic Serres.

Above right King George III, from a miniature by Richard Cosway.

Right The *Royal Charlotte*, flying the Royal Standard with her escorts *Mary* and *Katherine*, from a painting by Dominic Serres.

Napoleonic wars between 1794 and the Battle of Trafalgar in 1805, the returning fleets were welcomed by the King and his retinue. This was the time the Royal Navy became the formidable force it was to remain for a hundred years or more. Much of its power came from the long sea-time officers and men put in, far greater than their enemies, and from the peculiarly difficult conditions of sailing around the British Isles, which turned its sailors into seamen without equal.

In 1797, for instance, George III embarked on the *Royal Charlotte* to visit the fleet at Nore, at the mouth of the Thames, and to honour Admiral Duncan. Sadly the wind was blowing hard and against them, and the King was forced back up the river to Greenwich.

King George III is famous for having created a seaside resort out of Weymouth on the English south coast. Even during the wars

these excursions took place. In 1801 the *Augusta* made a voyage to Weymouth with the frigates *Hydra* and *Fortune* in attendance to prevent the very real danger of a surprise French attack. A contemporary account relates: 'The king went frequently to sea in his yacht. The two frigates kept close company and always passed the yacht on opposite tacks. To make the cruise pleasant the vessels were always beating, which ever way the wind was. The bands of music were always playing, and the thing was in many respects very agreeable.' This went on for a whole three months! Among the tunes most popular with the royal family was *Rule Britannia*, composed not long before. Its assertive lyrics would only take on their full meaning after the Battle of Trafalgar in 1805.

The principal royal yacht of this time, the aging *Royal Charlotte,* was replaced in 1804 by the *Royal Sovereign*, ship rigged with eight guns. Slightly larger than her forebear, at 96 feet, she was described as a very neat ship. Copper-bottomed and launched at Deptford, her stern carried some of the highly ornamented decorations we have come to associate with these earlier royal yachts. The figure of Neptune was prominent on her stern, with dolphins playing around him. Over the cabin windows and under the taffrail were figures from the four quarters of the world. Along her sides was an abundance of gingerbread. The *Royal Sovereign* proved to be a very fast ship, and the King used her for visits to Weymouth. In 1814 she took the exiled King Louis XVIII of France back from England across the Channel from Dover to Calais. She fell victim to the cuts imposed by the austerely reforming parliaments of the early 1830s and was converted to a depot ship. She was broken up in 1850.

In light of the madness of George III, in 1811 the Prince of Wales was declared Prince Regent, and two new royal yachts followed. The first, the *Prince Regent*, was laid down in 1815; she ended up as the official yacht for the Imam of Muscat, a gift from the British in 1836. The second was the *Royal George* (in which Queen Victoria was to make her only voyage in a royal yacht under sail). She lasted as a hulk until 1905. The last of the sailing-ship royal yachts was the second *Royal Charlotte*. Built in 1824 in Woolwich she only lasted until 1832, another victim of the move towards austerity which had one MP suggesting that if future monarchs wanted to go to sea they could do so in a warship. Issues of cost would rumble on, and these undertones of democratic changes would leave the future Queen Victoria permanently confused.

The *Royal George* made one major voyage after the accession to the throne of George IV in 1820. This was a tour of the British Isles and on to Hanover in 1821-22. As a sign of the times to come she was towed into Leith, in the Firth of Forth, by two steam packets.

This was to prove prophetic in more ways than one. The age of steam, on land and at sea, had dawned. After the quietitude of William IV in the 1830s, the age of Victoria would echo with the sound and fury of British, European and finally American mechanical industry. The young Queen was to be forever linked with all this progress in the spectacular era which took her name. In royal yachts there was to be a transformation too, and one insisted upon in the very beginning by a mere slip of a girl.

Left inset King George IV, from an engraving of 1828. His patronage of yachts and yacht racing gave it a boost it had not had since Charles II's day.

Below The *Royal George* with George IV on board coming to anchor in Portsmouth Harbour, from a painting by John T Serres.

CHAPTER 4

AT HEAVEN'S COMMAND

When Queen Victoria ascended the throne of Great Britain at the age of 18, in 1837, she could scarcely have begun to guess at the changes ahead which would lead to Britain dominating the world's trade by the time of her Golden Jubilee. The seeds of that domination had long been sown and were beginning to flower. The defeat of Napoleon at Trafalgar and at Waterloo had provided the means by which the *Pax Britannica* would enable all the countries of Europe to enjoy a hundred years of relative peace. For Britain, already well industrialised, full of invention and enthusiasm, ships and the trade that went with them, were the thick strands on which her economy would grow. Shipping in the nineteenth century was exciting in the way that steam railways were. Both were at the cutting edge of invention, much as aeroplanes are today; both carried elements of real danger. Ships, though, retained a romance long associated with the exotic. And ships, above all, remained the largest moving artefacts. It was perhaps inevitable, then, that the young Queen Victoria and her soon-to-be consort Prince Albert would be drawn to the maritime heart of the nation in a way not seen since Queen Elizabeth.

Queen Victoria had inherited a royal yacht, the *Royal George*, from the Regency period. She was 103 feet in length, 26-and-a-half feet in the beam, weighed 330 tons, and had been built at Deptford in 1817. She had carried George IV to Scotland in 1822. A description in the *Illustrated London News* of the day reports: 'The interior of the state cabin is superb, beautifully carved in the most prominent parts, and richly gilt, having a most pleasing effect. It is lighted by five windows in the stern, and two on each side of smaller dimensions, of the finest plate glass. Round the whole of the interior are placed ottomans and sofas, the latter convertible into beds, and by richly gilt rods, appearing at first

Detail left Queen Victoria at her Coronation. She grew to be the living symbol of the *Pax Britannica* giving reality to the 18th-century words of *Rule Britannia* . . .
When Britain first, at Heaven's command,
Arose from out the azure main,
This was the charter, the charter of the land,
And guardian angels sang the strain:
'Rule Britannia, Britannia rule the waves;
Britons never, never, never will be slaves.'

Below Queen Victoria and Prince Albert greeting the Emperor Louis Napoléon aboard the second *Victoria and Albert* at Boulogne in 1855.

supports for picture frames, curtains of graceful drapery are made to surround them. Near the stern windows is a beautiful brass stove, of a most elegant pattern, in the form of a handsome covered vase, the smoke descending behind the grate and finding egress at some distant part of the vessel. In recesses are neatly fitted shelves for book cases. The floor is covered with rich Brussels carpet of a very chaste pattern, and in the centre stands a splendidly-finished round mahogany table.

'The deck of the vessel is kept beautiful and clean, and being filled in the seams with a white, yet permanently hard composition, will not soil the most delicate shoe. The binnacle compass is covered in the form of a lantern, and surmounted by a royal crown. On the exterior of the stern is a beautifully carved royal arms, richly gilt.' Allowing some latitude for the writer's overuse of the word 'beautiful' we might generally surmise that the *Royal George* represented the finest of her kind. As it happens she was also the last of the great royal sailing ships, which had been used as transport for monarchs in one form or another for a century. She ended her days as accommodation for royal yacht crew, moored in Portsmouth harbour, and was finally broken up in 1905.

The technical revolution which had produced the fixed steam engine on land, mostly for pumping out mines, had also produced the first workable steam railway engines by the 1830s. Steam engines were also clearly destined for marine use; their large size was no particular problem for marine engineers, unlike the problems associated with reducing their size for railway engines. The greatest difficulties in the early days of ship use were the reluctance, centuries-old, of sailors to accept innovation, and their more understandable terror of fire at sea. The unreliability of the early marine engines and their paddle-box arrangements, helped to ensure that masts and sails would still figure prominently in ship design for decades to come.

But the marine steam engine had arrived, and sail, although always looking magnificent, had severe limitations, as Queen Victoria found when first she visited Scotland.

This visit, in August 1842, left from Woolwich, with the *Royal George* specially equipped with a new bed for Her Majesty. The 404

Above Queen Victoria and Prince Albert return from Scotland in the *Trident* in 1842, an unplanned voyage that was to prove of lasting significance.

nautical miles took a painful 66 hours, and involved some rather undignified towing by steam tugs in order to keep to the schedule. All this was witnessed by the large number of other craft manned by enthusiastic subjects following the royal fleet. For the young Queen it was particularly vexing to see her royal yacht passed on a number of occasions by paddle steamers. Arriving in Scotland she made it perfectly plain that she did not intend to have her subjects steal a march on her during the return journey. Her household hurriedly booked her homeward passage on the steamer *Trident.*

Queen Victoria had travelled with her Prime Minister, Sir Robert Peel (most famed for his 'invention' of the Metropolitan Police, or 'bobbies'). The day after they got back the Queen wrote to Peel. His reply, equally swift said: '...with reference to your Majesty's note of yesterday... the *first* act of Sir Robert Peel on his return from Scotland was to write to Lord Haddington [First Lord of the Admiralty] and strongly urge upon the Admiralty the necessity of providing a steam yacht for your Majesty's accommodation.' Peel mentioned that the Admiralty was experimenting with a screw-driven ship and that the shaking associated with paddle steamers appeared to be eliminated. He added that the Admiralty was also looking at ways to eliminate the smell from the smoke. We can be assured that the Queen, while expressing her desire to use steam-driven ships in her future travels, had also forcibly pointed out to the hapless Peel that she wanted less vibration and less smoke, on whatever that ship might be.

The royal yacht which was built on the back of these discussions was the first of three in the series named *Victoria and Albert.* Launched at Pembroke Dock in April 1843, she was just over 200 feet long, had a beam of 33 feet (59 feet over her paddle boxes), and a Thames Measurement tonnage of 1,049. She had one funnel and two masts. Her keel had been laid on the first birthday of the Prince of Wales, the future Edward VII, and her construction was unique for her time, consisting of overlapping planks set at 45 degrees to each other. She remained the premier royal yacht for 12 years. She was inspected by Prince Albert and the Lords of the Admiralty in the Thames on the 17th April 1843, before being fitted out and commissioned on 1st July.

The first *Victoria and Albert* became the prototype for hundreds of similar yachts, many of them for royalty across Europe and around the world. One of the key points about the monarchy in Britain at this time was that it set the fashion, not least because of Britain's increasing economic influence in a world communicating more and more. If the British Queen had a luxury steam yacht, then so would the crowned heads of the European nations.

In the past, royal yachts had been used for differing purposes. As we have seen, King Charles II used his for pleasure of the most innocent kind, cruising and racing them on the Thames. As time passed, they became important vehicles for the Georgian monarchs wishing to visit their relatives back in Hanover, or for travelling to various parts of the

British Isles during a period when the road system was virtually non-existent.

Queen Victoria was much more creative. Partly because she found a spiritual home on the Isle of Wight, at Osborne House, she needed ships for the numerous short crossings of the Solent. It is intriguing to recall, incidently, that Osborne House was paid for from the money saved by Prince Albert at Buckingham Palace – he insisted that candles be burned down to their ends, and that the household drank less of the monarch's wine. Osborne House is a rather ugly construction to be set in the sylvan grounds of the Isle of Wight, but it remained the Queen's favourite. She also had a palace – of rather more style – at Balmoral. It was Balmoral, along with discovering the Scottish Highlands (and thereby making them permanently fashionable), which caused her to travel north by yacht. She also voyaged to parts of Europe in this way, on the occasions she went to meet her many relatives.

Her most novel use of royal yachts was in her numerous cruises around the British Isles. She had a great advantage here in that there were hundreds of small commercial ports of vital economic importance for the bulk transport of goods, despite the growth of the railways.

Soon after the *Victoria and Albert* had been commissioned, the Queen undertook the first of these voyages, with Prince Albert. They embarked from Southampton in heavy rain, the Duke of Wellington helping her aboard. The royal yacht set off down Southampton Water followed by a large number of other vessels: naval, commercial and privately owned yachts. One of the naval guardships in attendance, the *Grecian,* had to have a steamer lashed to it, so that she could keep up with the royal yacht as it sailed off into the prevailing wind to Ryde on the Isle of Wight.

The following day the Queen and Prince Albert landed on the island. Confusion reigned as the royal party appeared to make a number of ad hoc excursions. The Royal Yacht Squadron, for example, was under the impression that the Queen would land there, and had put out the red carpet; in fact the royal barge passed on up the Medina and she landed outside the Medina Hotel near the Royal Thames Yacht Club in East Cowes. The Royal Yacht Squadron may never have recovered from this no doubt unintended slight.

From the Isle of Wight the royal yacht moved on via Weymouth and Dartmouth to Falmouth. At each stop the Queen was met by huge crowds, ashore and afloat – and by the mayors of the towns. One managed to fall overboard in his excitement, losing his mace as well as his dignity. The Queen's reaction is not recorded.

After Falmouth the *Victoria and Albert* crossed the Channel for a meeting with the King of France, Louis Philippe, at Tréport. During the Channel crossing the Queen, with a lady-in-waiting, was sitting by one of the paddle boxes, plaiting paper for bonnets – one of her favourite activities. She was approached by her Captain, Lord Adolphus Fitz-Clarence, who asked if she minded moving somewhere else. The Queen,

Above The *Victoria and Albert* in the Cove of Cork, during Queen Victoria's first visit to Ireland in 1849.

who had already remarked to her companion that she wondered why small groups of sailors had been gathering nearby muttering amongst themselves, nevertheless protested that she had chosen her spot so as to be out of the way.

'You are ma'am,' said Lord Adolphus, 'except you are sitting by the locker containing the men's grog and unless you move they may not have their ration.' The Queen agreed at once to move, but added she would do so only if she could have a tot of rum as well. When she had drunk it she is said to have told the sailors standing nearby that it would have been much better had it been stronger, a remark which caused much laughter.

The *Victoria and Albert* arrived at Tréport on 2nd September 1843, and the British royal party was met by the French King who went aboard. Among the party waiting ashore were the Queen of the Belgians as well as the Queen of France, the Duchess of Orléans, and Prince Augustus of Saxe-Coburg, a relative of Prince Albert. Four days at the Château Eu followed.

The Royal party then returned to Brighton, but was almost immediately off again, this time to Ostend and a meeting with Queen Victoria's beloved uncle, the King of the Belgians and his Queen. They continued on to Antwerp and the Scheldt estuary. How genuinely exciting it must have been, showing off a brand-new steam yacht to her European relatives and peers.

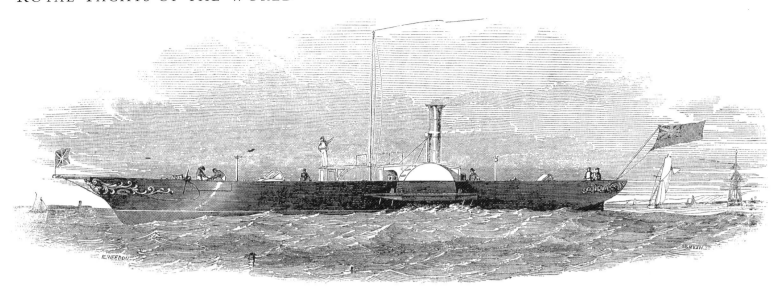

The *Victoria and Albert* was joined by the *Fairy*, a screw-driven ship built as a tender to her. Laid down at Blackwall in 1845, the *Fairy* was 146 feet long, had a beam of 21 feet and weighed 317 tons. She was replaced by the *Alberta* and dismantled in 1868. The *Fairy* was also used when the *Victoria and Albert* was unable to navigate the smaller rivers around the British coast.

These summer cruises, which might involve a cross-Channel voyage, or might consist of a visit to parts of the British Isles, became well-established. In 1846, for example, the Queen and the Prince went to Cornwall, then on to the Channel Islands; in 1847 they travelled to the Highlands of Scotland.

The summer cruise of 1847 was notable because the Queen later published an account of it in her own words, after Albert had died in 1861, as a memory of happier times. The cruise had a shaky start with fog in the Solent and rough weather along the south coast. They visited the Scilly Isles and stopped in Milford Haven on the Welsh coast. For 14th August the Queen wrote: 'We started at five o'clock, and the yacht then began to roll and pitch dreadfully, and I felt again very unwell; but I came on deck at three in the afternoon, the sea then was like glass, and we were close to the Welsh coast.

'This harbour, Milford Haven, is magnificent; the largest we have; a fleet might lie here. We are anchored just off Milford. Pembroke in front, in the distance. The cliffs, which are reddish brown are not very high. Albert and Charles went in the *Fairy* to Pembroke, and I sketched. Numbers of boats came out, with Welsh women in their curious high-crowned men's hats; and Bertie was much cheered, for the people seemed greatly pleased to see the "Prince of Wales".'

The royal party continued towards Scotland at a stately pace. On 16th August the Queen noted that 'something had gone wrong with the paddle wheel – just as happened last year – and it took full two hours to set it right.' Despite mishaps like these, the Queen was delighted with her views of Scotland from the sea. 'A bright fresh morning, the hills slightly tipped with clouds; a fine range of mountains splendidly lit up – green, pink, and lilac; the light on the hills was beautiful.'

Above The *Elfin* was launched at Chatham in 1849. She was later much in use as a despatch boat between Gosport and the Isle of Wight.

Inset right The renamed *Osborne* (formerly the first *Victoria and Albert*) was used by the Prince and Princess of Wales during a visit to Denmark and Sweden in 1864. She is here shown illuminated by fireworks at Elsinore.

Below right In 1865 the new royal yacht *Alberta*, a replacement for the *Fairy*, was used to take Queen Victoria down the River Thames to the Nore at the river's mouth.

The highlight of the voyage was probably the visit to Staffa, site of Fingals' Cave. The Queen wrote: 'At three we anchored close before Staffa, and immediately got into the barge with Charles, the children, and the rest of our people, and rowed towards the cave. As we rounded the point, the wonderful basaltic formation came into sight. The appearance it presents is most extraordinary; and when we turned the corner to go into the renowned Fingals' Cave, the effect was splendid, like a great entrance into a vaulted hall: it looked almost awful as we entered, and the barge heaved up and down on the swell of the sea. It is very high, but not longer than 227 feet, and narrower than I expected, being only 40 feet wide. The sea is immensely deep in the cave...' This was the first time the British Standard with a Queen of Great Britain, her husband and children had ever entered Fingals' Cave, and the men gave three cheers, which must have sounded very impressive.

In 1849, a further small royal yacht was added to the lists. The *Elfin* was built to run between Gosport and the Isle of Wight, following on from the Queen's decision to use Osborne House more or less as a second home. Built at Chatham Royal Dockyard, in the Medway, she was launched on 8th February 1849. It was a Mrs Allen who named her, sister of Mr Lang, the builder. The *Elfin* was 103 feet in length, 14 feet in the beam and drew 13 feet. She was to remain in service for many years. Her duties gradually evolved to include acting as a despatch boat for relaying government papers between the mainland and the Isle of Wight. Writing much later, Staff Captain Watts, her temporary Commander, explained: 'The duty of the *Elfin* was to leave Portsmouth, while the Queen was at Osborne, every weekday about 10 o'clock with the London papers and official letters for Osborne, landing them at Osborne Bay (which was close to East Cowes); leave Cowes at about 2.00pm with the Queen's messenger, taking him to Southampton with government dispatches, land him there and embark another, taking him to Cowes and remaining there till 7.00pm the next day, when she proceeded to Portsmouth, to leave again at 10.00am.' Locally, she became known as the milk boat. She was finally broken up in 1901.

The British monarchy of course had been re-established for centuries after the turmoil of the Civil War. As we have seen, had it not been for that tumultuous time, the very idea of royal yachts might never have emerged in the way it did. By the nineteenth century, many European countries had equally well-established royal families, most of which were related to – or would become related to – Queen Victoria and her expanding family. As for early steam royal yachts, the British lagged behind one other European neighbour – the Dutch.

De Leeuw (the Lion), the Dutch royal yacht of the early part of the nineteenth century, had been built in Rotterdam in 1826 to designs by P Glavimans. In length 120 feet, beam 18-and-a-half feet, and drawing six-and-a-half feet, she was a wooden-hulled paddle steamer, with two masts but no sails. Her engine was the simplest oscillating type, producing 25 hp.

The Dutch had introduced a constitutional monarchy as an experiment in 1814 and William I had become King of a country that still included Belgium. (Belgium broke away in 1830, forming another constitutional monarchy on British lines.)

De Leeuw was built for the second Dutch King, William II. Once launched she was the first steam-driven royal yacht in Europe, although she was a very modest size. She followed Dutch tradition in having extremely ornate decoration. Much of this was concentrated around her paddle boxes, a symbol of progress. The tall, narrow funnel had to be well stayed. She remained in service for 55 years and she was often used as a tender for larger vessels.

In 1846 a schooner was launched at East Cowes for the Tsar of Russia Nicholas I. Named the *Queen Victoria*, at his request, she was 95 feet long, had a beam of 22 feet and drew 12 feet. The Grand Duke Constantine was due to launch the yacht in the presence of Queen Victoria, but as it turned out, the *Victoria and Albert* on which the Grand Duke and the Queen were arriving was delayed, so the ceremony went ahead without them! In the end the wife of the Russian consul broke a bottle of Lacryma Christi wine on her bow.

The Grand Duke turned up a day or so later and inspected the yacht for his father. The yacht had been designed by Mr White, who had previously designed and built two great classic yachts, *Water Witch* and *Daring*, and the Tsar had become aware of both of these and wished to have a yacht on the same lines. The commission came via the Commodore of the Royal Western Yacht Club, Lord Mount Edgecumbe, who had not been aware at the time for whom it was ultimately destined. It was initially crewed by Welshmen with an English skipper, Mr Powell.

If the Tsar of all the Russias was indulging himself with a fine racing yacht, the Danish king had been provided with an ex-North Sea ferry for his official yacht. The *Slesvig* had been built by Robert Napier in 1845 as the *Copenhagen*, used between the Baltic ports of Kiel and Copenhagen. In length almost 176 feet, beam 26-and-a-half feet, and drawing eight feet, she was rigged as a three-masted schooner. Her engines were steam, Napier side-lever, providing 240 nautical horse power and a top speed of 10 knots. Her paddle wheels were over 42 feet in diameter. She had been first acquired by the Danish Navy in 1848, and renamed the *Slesvig*; as a naval vessel she variously plied as a tug and

Below The steam yacht *Falkin* built for Frederick VII, King of Denmark, in 1858.

as a troop transport. In 1856 King Christian IX approved her as a royal yacht and she stayed in use as such until 1879. She was broken up in 1894, having been taken off the Navy List as a royal yacht in 1879. Much like the *Victoria and Albert,* she provided this Scandinavian monarchy with much pleasure down the years. One of their offspring, Princess Alexandra, had by then married the British Prince of Wales and would, one day, have a British royal yacht named after her – the *Alexandra.*

In 1858 the Danish King, Frederick VII, acquired a second royal yacht, the *Falkin,* designed and built by Charles Langley of Deptford. She was 127 feet long, 19 feet in beam and drew 11-and-a-half feet. Her tonnage was 195. Built of iron she was a copy of the ships that were then being used to carry the mails from England to the Cape colonies in South Africa.

Also in 1858 the Austrian Emperor had a yacht built for his brother, the Grand Duke Maximilian. The *Fantasie* was laid down by the Thames Shipbuilding Company from designs by James Ash. She was driven by a 120 hp engine built by George Rennie and Sons of Southwark. Her overall length was 169 feet, she had a beam of 18 feet and drew 11 feet, weighing in at 291 tons. She was described at the time as 'the most perfect model of nautical beauty that has yet appeared in the Thames, and is of finer lines than are possessed by the celebrated Dover and Ostend mail-packet, *Prince Frederick-William,* one of the fastest boats in the world.' The *Fantasie* had after-cabins for the use of the Duke and Duchess, and a 'splendid' saloon with couches on each side and mirrors at either end, with sleeping cabinets, library and

Below The steam yacht *Fantasie* built for the Emperor of Austria in 1858.

bathroom, all decorated in white enamel and gold. A 'handsome' staircase led to a deckhouse. She carried two 25-foot cutters built by Searle of Standgate, lowered by means of Clifford's patented boat-lowering apparatus.

The French had a very on-off love affair with monarchy in the nineteenth century. It had started with Napoléon making the fatal mistake, in the view of many, proclaiming himself Emperor. Although largely preoccupied with his armies and fighting across Europe, Napoléon did order a state barge to be built in 1811. *Le Canot Impérial* was 56 feet long, almost 11 feet in beam and required 26 oarsmen. She was built in only three weeks, and her first avowed purpose was for an inspection of the defences of the port of Antwerp. She was elaborately decorated at the bow with Neptune astride a sea beast, cherubs all around. Her saloon, built aft, was of a classically simple design. In the middle of the Second World War *Le Canot Impérial* was brought to Paris to the Musée Marine at the Palais de Chaillot, where she remains to this day.

It was the last royal family in France, that of Napoléon III and the Empress Eugénie, who built the only proper royal yachts ever owned by that country. The first of these was *L'Aigle,* built in 1858. Another paddle steamer, she was rigged as a three-masted schooner, 160 feet in length, 25 feet in the beam and drawing about 10 feet. Louis Napoléon had declared himself Emperor of France in 1852 after a *coup d'état.* Despite its uneasy origins, the Second Empire in France was a period of great development in which railways and industry boomed, as did French

Below The first steam yacht built for the Emperor Napoléon III of France, *L'Aigle,* seen at the opening of the Suez Canal in 1869. Empress Eugénie was on board.

shipbuilding. *L'Aigle* was part of these developments. She was by all accounts a reliable and comfortable vessel, her black hull ornamented with gilding at her eagle figurehead and along the moulded strakes running the length of her hull. She also sported imitation gunports – in reality shuttered portholes. Napoléon III made many cruises in her including a visit to Venice.

Above The steam yacht *Jérôme Napoléon* built for Prince Napoléon in 1866.

Right The armed steam yacht *Immacolata Concezione* built for the private use of the Pope in 1859.

The *Jérôme Napoléon* was second in this series, named for the Emperor's cousin. She was built at Le Havre in 1866 by MA Normand. Iron-hulled and rigged as a barquentine, she had a length of 285 feet, a beam of 22 feet and drew 18 feet. She was powered by a three-cylinder steam reciprocating engine of 450 hp built by the Mazeline Brothers. In her trials she made over 15 knots. Contemporary accounts say she was very impressive, and looked every inch like a warship. There is a possibility that this yacht was used by Prince Jérôme when he arrived in Turin in 1859 for his marriage to the 15-year-old daughter of King Victor Emmanuel of Piedmont and Sardinia. The married couple are likely to have used the yacht for their honeymoon.

The third French royal yacht was *Le Reine Hortense*. She was built at Le Havre as the *Patriote*, then renamed the *Comte d'Eu*; she finally appears as *La Reine Hortense* in 1867. Not very much is known about her except that she was probably wooden. She may well have come to Cowes with the Emperor on board: he was a member of the Royal Yacht Squadron.

Perhaps it should come as no surprise that in all the excitement being engendered by royal yachts, one should have been built for the Pope. What might be more surprising was that she was armed. *Immacolata Concezione* was laid down by the Thames Iron and Shipbuilding Company from designs by James Ash in 1859. Her engines were from Messrs J Seaward and Co of Millwall. A full 178 feet long, with a beam of 27 feet and drawing 16 feet, she weighed 627 tons. Her engines provided 160 hp, and she had an average speed of 12-and-a-half knots. Built for the Pope's private use, she was armed with eight brass 18-pounder guns. The fitting out, it was reported at the time, was of the highest order and 'the private cabin for His Holiness a model of taste and elegance'. Little is known of this vessel once she had completed her trials on the Thames and had been sailed away to the Papal State in Italy. She was probably based in Naples, but whether she was ever used by pontiffs who, in the nineteenth century rarely ventured away from Rome, is not known.

By the mid 1850s the three British royal vessels were joined by a fourth. It was built as a replacement for the *Victoria and Albert* whose furthest voyage had been to Gibraltar, but without any royalty aboard. The second *Victoria and Albert* was a much larger ship, first called the *Windsor Castle* but renamed the *Victoria and Albert II* by order of the Queen. Confusingly, the old *Victoria and Albert* was then briefly called the *Windsor Castle* before being renamed the *Osborne*. The *Victoria and Albert II* was the apotheosis of the classic Victorian steam paddle yacht, and she became the Queen's favourite. She remained the chief British royal yacht for 40 years.

On her deck she had two large 'tea houses', and there were two six-pound guns for signalling. Her upper deck was laid with linoleum, not teak, although a carpet was laid when the Queen was on board. In 1888, after much protest from the elderly Queen, she was given electric lights.

The royal apartments aft used a good deal of chintz at the specific insistence of Prince Albert, who involved himself a great deal in the interior design. The Queen's bedroom, 19 feet by 14 feet, had a dressing room at each end. The Queen's drawing room was 26 feet by 18-and-a-half feet. The sides were covered with chintz, and the hanging pictures were of the royal family in oval gilt frames. The furniture was of bird's-eye maple, also with chintz coverings. There were two large sofas, one at each end of the room, two or three easy chairs, with others high-backed. There was an Erard piano, a bookcase with cabinet combined, writing tables, and an oval centre table. The cabins were ventilated by pipes passing up through the ship's sides to the gunwales.

Above Queen Victoria invests Abdul Aziz, Sultan of Turkey, with the Order of the Garter, on board *Victoria and Albert II* in Cowes Roads, 1867.

On the state deck, on both port and starboard sides, wing passages ran under the shafts of the paddle wheels connecting the royal apartments aft with the royal household and the officers' quarters forward. These became favourite playgrounds for the royal children and grandchildren of Queen Victoria. Between the state cabins and apartments there was a wide corridor joining the upper deck via a spacious stairway, leading to the lobby of the dining room. Cabins on the starboard side, from forward going aft, were the Queen's wardrobe room, the Queen's and Prince's bedroom, the Prince's dressing room, then cabins for the Princess Royal, the governess and dresser. Right aft came the breakfast room with a square stern and sideports.

On the port side from forward were the drawing room, the cabins of the Prince of Wales and his tutor, a valet's cabin, bathroom and royal pantry. All the royal apartments were covered with red-and-black Brussels carpets. The walls were hung with box-pleated rosebud chintz. The doors had ivory handles with electro-plated fittings; the doors themselves were of bird's-eye maple.

Forward of the paddle boxes were more apartments for the royal household – ladies-in-waiting on the starboard side, lords-in-waiting

on the port. The officers and crew occupied a very cramped set of quarters forward.

She was launched at Pembroke Dock on the 16th January 1854. Designed by O Lang, she was 336 feet long, had a beam of 40 feet and drew 24 feet. Her Thames tonnage was 2,470 and her engines could produce nearly 3,000 hp, giving her a top speed of 15 knots. The *Illustrated London News*, covering the launch, pointed out that she was about as long as the 'great' *Himalaya*, then the biggest steamship afloat. She was built on the diagonal principle, to combine lightness with strength, mostly of mahogany and East India teak. Her decks were laid with Canadian fir planks and there were watertight bulkheads set against the royal apartments. Felt was laid between the beams and the deck to deaden sound.

The dockyard had hoped that the Queen might attend the launch, but the ship had to make way for a new battleship on the slip, the *Alma*, and so a January date had to be set, when the Queen was unavailable. Instead the *Victoria and Albert II* was sent on her way by Lady Milford, at 4pm, under threatening skies; a large crowd had gathered to watch. Fitted out at speed, her first voyage with the royal family was in the following July, around the Isle of Wight. In August 1854 she crossed the Channel with the Queen and Prince Albert, on a visit to the Emperor Napoléon.

Queen Victoria lent the *Victoria and Albert II* to the Empress of Austria in 1860 for what turned out to be a very rough crossing from mainland Europe to Madeira. She remained there through that winter returning to England via Trieste and Gibraltar the following spring. This was the only time she ever entered the Mediterranean. Her use after 1861 was erratic.

Prince Albert died, probably of stomach cancer, in December 1861, and thereafter the Queen was in a state of permanent mourning. The yacht was used in 1863 to bring Princess Alexandra from Denmark to Britain for her marriage to the Prince of Wales.

Meanwhile the *Fairy* had been replaced by the *Alberta* in 1863 as the tender to the *Victoria and Albert II*. She was a wooden-built paddle steamer, also out of Pembroke Dock, with two funnels and three masts. In length 160 feet, in beam 23 feet, she had a displacement tonnage of 370. She was finally broken up in 1913. In August 1865, Queen Victoria used her for a visit to Germany. A contemporary account published in the *Illustrated London News* says: 'It was in the evening, at twenty minutes to seven, when the *Alberta*, conveying her Majesty and the Princesses Louisa, Helena, and Beatrice, attended by Earl Granville, General Grey, the Duchess of Roxburghe, and Lady Churchill, with some of the officers of the Royal household, left Woolwich and steamed down the river. She joined the *Victoria and Albert* just below the Chapman, since the evening was very fine, and her Majesty preferred to make the passage down the Thames in the lighter vessel.' The two royal yachts then crossed to Antwerp where the royal party joined a train to travel on to Coburg, home to the then late Prince Albert's family.

Interest in steam yachts for regal purposes had quickly spread far beyond the shores of Europe. In March 1847, at Cowes, a steam yacht for the Grand Sultan of Turkey was launched. The *Vassitei Tiidjaret* was sent on her way from the slip she had been built on by Her Highness Princess Callimaki, the 'lady' of the Turkish Ambassador (so described by the *Illustrated London News* with a fine sense of decorum, given the Victorians' understanding of the polygamous nature of Turkish society). She was 210 feet long, had a beam of 52 feet over her paddle boxes and drew 20 feet. Her engines were by Maudsley and produced 340 hp. Her name means 'medium of commerce', and although she was to be used as a private yacht by the Sultan, Abdul Medjid Khan, the Turkish Government, on whose orders she had been built, decreed that she was also to be occasionally used as a mail packet between Constantinople (modern Istanbul) and Trebizonde in the Black Sea. The yacht had a 45-foot state saloon and 26 other private guest rooms. Her figurehead was a dragon, and on her stern was 'emblazoned' in gilt a crescent moon and star.

She was followed shortly after by the *Sayed Pacha*, built for Egyptian 'royalty' in the portly shape of her namesake, Sayed Pacha, the eldest surviving son of the renowned Mohammed Ali, and thus heir presumptive to the Viceroyalty of Egypt. The *Sayed Pacha* was laid down at Greenock, by Messrs Caird and Company, under the direction of Messrs Galloway of Alexandria and London. She was 156 feet long, had a beam of 17 feet, but drew only two-and-a-half feet so she could navigate the shallow waters of the Nile. Her oscillating engines produced a feeble 80 hp although they had been 'worked' to 120 hp. Her paddles could be 'feathered' to eliminate drag in the water when not being turned by the engines. She carried three masts.

Below The *Sayed Pacha* was built in 1849 for the private use of Sayed Pacha, Grand Admiral of the Egyptian Fleet, eldest son of Mohammed Ali and heir to the Viceroyalty of Egypt.

Below The elegant and graceful *Said* built for Sayed Pacha in 1858, by then the Viceroy of Egypt.

Above The new Viceroy's son Hami Pasha had the *Cleopatra* built in 1858.

The main royal saloon was nearly 60 feet long and, as usual, aft. From it led a metal staircase up to the deck and into a charmingly small, round house with stained-glass windows. Externally she was decorated with Egyptian figures in gilt, with a variety of gingerbread scrollwork along her sides.

One novelty was her steam whistle which could produce music, rather than just a hoot. As a contemporary said, with more than a hint that this was Eastern vulgarity, it merely proved the 'oft-quoted remark that everything will be done by steam'. The same voice, however, pointed out that Sayed Pacha had shown his good taste in other respects by patronising British art, science and manufacture – 'an indisputable proof of his enlightened ideas'.

Nine years later, and ensconced as the Viceroy, Sayed Pacha proved his good taste once more by ordering a new iron-screw steam yacht, the *Said*. She was said to be 'of exceedingly elegant and graceful proportions, her lines very fine fore and aft'. Overall her length was 250 feet, her beam 28 feet and she displaced 900 tons. *Said* was rigged as a three-masted schooner. Her engines could produce 250 hp. Her masts and spars were varnished, the deck metalwork was of brass, the woodwork of teak and oak, both highly polished. She had two funnels, painted white, and a shield figurehead on which were the crescent and stars of her owner's coat of arms, in gold on a silver background. A gold line ran right round the ship; her elliptical stern was carved.

Internally, her main saloon was 40 feet long with a breadth of 25 feet. The floor in this saloon was made of papier mâché prepared in such a way as to prolong its life. The settees were covered with figured silk damask of blue and silver. Running around three sides of the saloon were embossed mirrors; on the fourth side was one huge mirror split by two doors leading off to staircases and to bathrooms. In the centre of the saloon floor was a fountain of papier mâché and glass. In the harem there was a speed indicator, a steam gauge and a clock, also fitted in papier mâché casings.

The Viceroy's son, Il Hami Pasha, also had had a yacht built for himself, the *Cleopatra*, about which little is known. But when his father died and he acceded to the throne, his new grand yacht was the *Faid Gihaad*. She was a paddle steamer, 383 feet long in an uninterrupted flush deck, and at that time the largest vessel ever to have come up the Thames. Her original length had been 69 feet less, but she had been modified by Forresters of Liverpool. The quarterdeck was covered with a floorcloth and was screened off by a white canvas awning. The saloons

Below The *Faid Gihaad* was built in 1862 for the new Viceroy of Egypt.

were fitted out with great splendour; the supports of silver gilt and the panelling and decoration were very elaborate. The state bed was emblazoned at either end with a gilded representation of the rising and setting sun. The Egyptian emblem – the crescent – was worked into the ship at every conceivable point.

If the Egyptian Viceroys and their families were indulging themselves, so were the Turkish sultans. In January 1864, the *Taliah*, the new imperial yacht for the Sultan, by Samuda Brothers of Poplar, east London, had made her trial run from Tilbury Fort on the Thames to the Nore and the river mouth. She had reached the astonishing speed of 16.2 knots against the tide, 19.25 knots with it – an average of 17.75 knots or 20.5 mph. It made her among the very fastest ships then afloat. Witnesses noted at the time that she was as fast as a railway train. The engines that accomplished this amazing feat were built with a double set of boilers and a nominal horsepower of 350, although on this trial, with the Turkish Ambassador on board, she is said to have attained an incredible 2,700 hp. It was, apparently, hard to keep your hat on while standing on deck, even in a calm.

But the Samuda Brothers had had a greater triumph. She was the *Mahroussa*. Laid down in 1865 and launched in 1866, the iron-hulled *Mahroussa* in her first manifestation was a paddle steamer; in 1905 she was lengthened to 420 feet with a beam of nearly 43 feet. She drew 17-and-a-half feet and had a gross tonnage of 3,762. During this refit her paddle-wheel propulsion was removed and she was given triple-screw steam turbines. Rumour has it that today these engines have been replaced again – with gas turbines! She remains not only one of the

largest royal yachts ever built but also certainly the oldest afloat, living out her days as a training ship for the Egyptian Navy after four engine changes and countless modifications.

By the mid 1850s the world was being opened up to a flood of European interest no longer confined to intrepid explorers. Trade, trade and more trade was transforming all aspects of life. As it developed so did a general European interest in the exotic. Little at the time was more exotic than the Far East – those places beyond India and the increasingly British-dominated subcontinent. Siam (modern Thailand) and Japan were two of those places.

The Chief Officer of the barque *Gleaner* recounted a voyage he had made to the court of the Kings of Siam in 1857. After remarking that Bangkok was a curious town in which 'two-thirds of the houses are afloat', Chief Officer Chevalier was introduced to the royal family, shaking hands with the 'Second' King. 'The Siamese have a First and a Second King,' he wrote. 'Two or three times a week they visit the temples, the procession to which is a grand sight. The Royal barges are long canoes, splendidly ornamented in gold and silver. The First King is

Above and inset In 1866 a luxurious state yacht, the *Mahroussa*, was built for the Viceroy. She was still afloat in 1997 in a stretched and rebuilt hull, a training ship but occasionally of use as the Egyptian presidential yacht.

paddled by upwards of 100 men followed by the Second King's and numerous others of the Royal family and higher class, bands soldiers, etc.. On these days all shops etc., are closed. The natives have to kneel, keeping their heads towards the ground, as the procession goes past their houses. The First King is rather old, all management being left to the Second, who is a smart active intelligent man, always seeking to improve and advance the trade of his country and manners of his subjects: he is very fond of navigation.'

If Siam were thought by the West to be exotic, Japan was treated as if it were on another planet. The Japanese had spent centuries deliberately keeping foreigners at bay and it was only in the mid nineteenth century that the Meiji regime found it had to bow to the inevitable – Western influence. The US Navy Commander Perry's black ships had steamed into Tokyo Bay in 1853; soon the Japanese would be forced into concluding treaties with the Americans, the British and the French. The British, at least, offered gifts as well as threats, one of which was a yacht for the Japanese emperor. Named *The Emperor*, and built on the

Below Royal barges of the Kings of Siam from the mid 1850s. The barges were splendidly ornamented in gold and silver and paddled by many oarsmen.

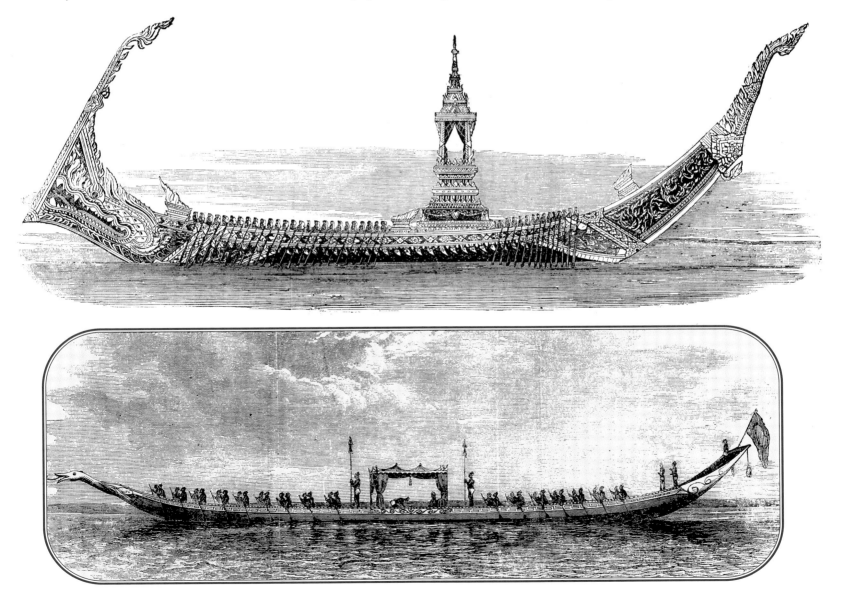

Above The steam yacht *The Emperor* built by the British government for presentation to the Emperor of Japan.

Thames, she was financed out of £10,000 voted in the Royal Navy estimates. She was of 300 tons and wooden, and given engines by Penn, somewhat less powerful than the *Taliah*, at just 60 hp. She was sailed to Japan by a British crew in 1857.

In 1859 the King of Ava (part of modern Burma, now Myanmar) ordered his pleasure yacht from Napier and Son, in Glasgow. She was 190 feet long, had a beam of 18 feet and drew eight feet. She had a spoon-shaped bow and stern to fit the oddities of navigating the Irawaddy. She was propelled by a pair of oscillating engines driving paddle wheels. She was shipped out to Rangoon in parts, and reassembled there. Externally, her hull was decorated with ornamental mouldings in white metal; the stern and paddle boxes had carved work, each carrying as a centrepiece a peacock, the emblem of Burmese royalty. Internally, she was opulently fitted out in bird's-eye maple, tulip wood and plate glass (then a huge novelty). The King of Ava was a great admirer of the British – he had recently contributed £1,000 to the Indian Relief Fund. Buying a British yacht, however, was not about sentiment: the British were rapidly cornering the market in steam yachts and, as such, their designs were the best, as indeed they were generally in ships and shipping.

The huge expansion of the British merchant fleet was in part matched by other European countries, notably France and Italy. Many of these ships plied the Middle and Far Eastern seas and had to make the long voyage around the southern tip of Africa. Passengers went via the Mediterranean, transferring to a train to cross the desert from the Mediterranean to the Red Sea then embarking once more on a ship.

The plan to build a canal to link the Mediterranean Sea with the Red Sea might be likened to the building in the late 1980s of the tunnel under the English Channel: both were technically feasible yet proved to be at the limits of what could be done in civil engineering for their time. Both excited public imagination. The Prince and Princess of Wales had visited the works in Egypt on board the *Osborne* (previously the first *Victoria and Albert*). But, at the opening ceremony of the Suez Canal in November 1869, it was the French royal yacht *L'Aigle* that stole the show. The Empress Eugénie was the French representative-in-chief, there to celebrate their man, Ferdinand de Lesseps, who had masterminded the whole project. *L'Aigle* received a warm welcome from a British fleet of battleships. The Austrian Emperor aboard *Fantasie*, and the Viceroy of Egypt aboard the magnificent *Mahroussa*, completed the party of luminaries. It was noted that among the array of shipping from Britain, France, Austria, Italy, Russia and many other nations, there was none from America. But at that time the USA hardly had an ocean-going merchant fleet at all, relying on the British instead.

It was *L'Aigle,* with the Empress Eugénie on board, which became the first vessel to sail through the Suez Canal. She was followed by *Fantasie* with the Austrian Emperor; a Prussian frigate with the Crown Prince on board; the Swedish royal yacht *Drott*, with Prince Oscar; then a Russian warship with the Grand Duke Michael; the Russian Admiral's ship; a Dutch gunboat with a prince and princess from Holland; then *Psyche*, a British despatch boat with the British Ambassador from Constantinople.

The opening of the Suez Canal marks an important moment in world maritime history, and it was fitting that so many royal yachts should have been present. Their apogee had yet to come, however, both in terms of design and of grandeur.

Below The steam pleasure-yacht of the King of Ava in 1859.

CHAPTER **5**

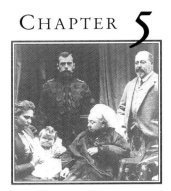

APOTHEOSIS
THE GOLDEN AGE OF ROYAL YACHTS
1870–1914

The *Victoria and Albert II* had been used extensively by the Queen until Prince Albert's death in 1861. Thereafter the ship's voyages were largely restricted to the British Isles. However, in 1868 she cruised along the Norwegian coast with the German Princess Leiningen and, in 1870, she undertook a lengthy cruise in the Baltic with the Prince and Princess of Wales. In 1878 Queen Victoria sailed with the Duke of Connaught, her third son, on a tour of inspection of Heligoland in the North Sea, then still a British colony, before continuing on to visit the German Emperor in Hamburg. Finally, in 1896, she returned to the Baltic with the Duke and Duchess of Connaught, when they attended the Coronation of Tsar Nicholas II.

In 1863, to revisit one earlier voyage not long after Prince Albert's death, the *Victoria and Albert II* crossed to the Dutch port of Flushing, to bring back the bride-to-be of the Prince of Wales. The Danish Princess Alexandra found her cabin filled with roses sent by the Prince. Warships, including the *Warrior* and the *Revenge,* were part of the escort back to Britain. The crossing was unusually smooth and they reached the Nore on 6th March. At Margate on the north Kent coast, where the yacht anchored for the night, the Princess received an address of welcome from the Mayor and Corporation, and the admirals and captains of the British fleet were presented to her. Southend and Sheerness, those unprepossessing towns at the mouth of the Thames, got out their illuminations for her, and bonfires blazed on the shores. Sheerness went so far as to organise blue lights, 10 feet high, that spelled

Detail above Queen Victoria pictured with the Prince of Wales (later King Edward VII), Tsar Nicholas II of Russia, his wife Alexandra (granddaughter of Victoria) and their daughter Olga.

Right The *Victoria and Albert II,* Queen Victoria's favourite ship and one that served her for 47 years.

'welcome'. The modest Princess from Denmark was overwhelmed. 'Are all these things for me?' she asked her mother. One cannot but help be reminded of similar celebrations in 1981, 120 years on, for another marriage of a British heir to the throne. That too involved a young girl swept up in a tidal wave of national emotion. Prince Edward and Princess Alexandra were married four days later on 10th March 1863. Later that same day the couple managed to arrive at Southampton and embarked on the *Fairy*, to spend the first part of their honeymoon at Osborne House.

In 1874 a new yacht was commissioned. The *Osborne* (the second one) was built to replace the first which had been broken up in 1868, and she continued in service until 1908 (when she herself was replaced by the *Alexandra*). The *Osborne* was used a great deal by the Prince and Princess of Wales for cruises in the Mediterranean and for sailing at Cowes Week in August each year. By now, the Prince of Wales, as well as embracing actresses, had fallen head over heels in love with yachting.

One of the more curious events with which the *Osborne* was connected was the report by her Captain in 1877, during one of the Mediterranean cruises, that a sea serpent had been sighted off the coast of Sicily. At 5pm on 2nd June, Captain Pearson said that he and two fellow officers 'saw a head, two flappers, and about thirty feet of an animal's shoulders. The head was about six feet thick, the neck narrower, about four to five feet; the shoulders about fifteen feet across, the flappers about fifteen feet in length'. Lieutenant Forsyth described

Left The Prince of Wales' steam yacht *Osborne,* a replacement for her namesake, and used a great deal at Cowes Week and for cruises in the Mediterranean.

it as 'a huge monster, having a head about fifteen to twenty feet in length; the head was round, and full at the crown. The animal was swimming in a south-easterly direction, propelling itself by means of two large flappers or fins'. Three observations, made by telescope in daylight at 400 yards, by trained naval personnel, suggest they must have seen something very unusual. We might assume, too, that they wouldn't have mistaken this creature for any kind of whale, with which they all would have been familiar.

Her next Commander, Lord Charles Beresford, looked after the *Osborne* from 1879 to 1881. She was commissioned for only a few months each year. There were trips to Denmark including many shooting parties. Lord Beresford wrote of one of these: 'I was the only person present who was not either a King actual or a King prospective. There were the King of Denmark, the King of Norway and Sweden, and the King of Greece, the Prince of Wales, the Cesarewitch [Tsarevich], the Crown Princes of Denmark, of Norway and Sweden, and Greece.' Lord Beresford's short time with a royal yacht was unusual – most officers and men stayed for many years. But Beresford wanted to move

Below The *Alberta* off Cowes in 1901, a familiar sight on the Solent.

around more, and he requested a transfer. The Queen was bothered by this, telling him that she hoped he wasn't about to suggest the same should happen with the rest of the officers. 'I am an old woman now, and I like to see faces I know about me, and not have to begin again with new faces,' she told him.

In August 1875 the Queen was returning from Osborne on the *Alberta* when it was in collision with the schooner *Mistletoe*. The Captain of the *Alberta* had altered course to pass behind the *Mistletoe*, but she suddenly tacked and they ran into her. The Queen's diary provides a graphic account. 'This has been an eventful day, and one of terrible and undying recollections! At half past five left dear Osborne, with Beatrice and Leopold, and embarked at Trinity Pier. The evening was very fine, so bright, and no wind. The *Victoria and Albert* followed us. When we neared Stokes Bay, Beatrice said very calmly, "Mama, there is a yacht coming against us," and I saw the tall masts and large sails of a schooner looming over us. In an instant came an awful, most terrifying crash, accompanied by a very severe shake and reel. Horatia and Harriet came running and saying there had been a collision, and at the same time General Ponsonby and Lord Bridport rushed up saying, "There is no danger." A frightful alarm seized me lest some of our people, who always stand in the bows of the vessel, might get hurt. I was assured, however, they were all safe, and Leopold came round at the same moment, so that I knew nothing had happened to him.

'It all took only a few seconds, and, when I enquired to whom the yacht belonged, I was told she had gone down! In great distress I said, "Take everyone, take everyone on board," repeating this several times. I then went forward, to where all the excitement had been going on, and was horrified to find not a single vestige of the yacht, merely a few spars and deck chairs floating about. Two boats were moving around, and we saw one of our men swimming about with a life-belt, and one poor man in the water, who was pulled into the barge, nearly drowned, with his face quite black. I saw no others in the water, but on deck three or four yachtsmen, also a lady, looking anxiously from one side to the other. These had jumped across from the sinking yacht on to the *Alberta*. At first it was hoped that everyone had been saved, and General Ponsonby said the numbers were being counted. Alas! then it became clear that one lady, whom Leopold had distinctly seen on the deck with the other, was missing, also one man – a dreadful moment.'

The Queen comforted the woman on deck. 'Her expression was heart-rending to see,' she noted. When they reached Gosport the Queen sent for her General to tell him that the greatest care should be taken of the survivors. It was subsequently established that both the master and two passengers of the *Mistletoe* had been killed in this accident. At the coroner's inquest held into the two deaths the jury could not reach a verdict. The principal unresolved question was how fast the *Alberta* had been travelling when the two ships collided, and what action each vessel ought to have taken.

In the same year as this accident, the Prince of Wales had travelled to India in the *Serapis*, an Indian troopship which accompanied the *Osborne.* In the Suez Canal the Prince transferred to the *Osborne* for a visit to the Khedive at Ismailiya. The Prince spent four months in India. Then on his return he embarked on the *Osborne* at Gibraltar, calling at Cadiz for a visit to the Kings of Spain and of Portugal; he re-embarked in the *Serapis* at Lisbon. On 11th May the royal fleet reached the Needles where Princess Alexandra and their children awaited their father in the Admiralty yacht *Enchantress*.

In her old age the Queen travelled abroad again, to Italy and to the French Riviera. She insisted she was sufficiently incognito, and always expressed surprise, as her train passed through France, that local dignitaries turned out to greet her. These holidays began on one or other of the royal yachts, taking her across the Channel. In 1879, the year in which her son, the Duke of Connaught, married Princess Frederick Charles of Prussia, the Queen and Princess Beatrice left for Cherbourg in the *Osborne*. The passage was rough, snow falling. By now the Queen had as a close consort the Scottish former ghillie, John Brown, subject of much speculation. (She had been frequently referred to as Mrs Brown by some newspapers.) Brown was a constant visitor to the bridge on this voyage, asking each time if the weather was going to

Above HMS Serapis, a troopship refitted for the voyage of the Prince of Wales to India in 1875. The *Serapis* was accompanied by the *Osborne*.

Above Victoria and Albert II in 1899, near the end of a long and distinguished career.

improve because, he said: 'the puir boddie downstairs does not feel at all well'. The same 'puir wee boddie' could still exercise her queenly wrath, as on another occasion, in the following year, when she threw a pile of local dignitaries off the *Victoria and Albert II.* They had dared to come aboard as soon as the gangplank had gone down, hoping to wish her well. Another trip, when her children wanted to take a short cruise on the *Osborne,* only got started when one of them was sent to the Queen to ask if they could go – no-one had previously thought to get her express permission.

In such ways the final years of the great Queen's reign passed. In December 1882, the *Alberta* took her to Stokes Bay near Gosport on the mainland side of the Solent. She landed to visit the wounded at Haslar Hospital, back from yet another interminable colonial war, this one in Egypt. In 1883, the *Victoria and Albert II* underwent a two-year refit, and the Queen used the *Osborne,* which she is said to have liked much less, especially for Channel crossings. In 1884, that same yacht was sent to Cherbourg, her gilt work covered in black, to bring home the remains of Prince Leopold, the Queen's fourth son, who had died at Cannes. In 1885, newly refitted, the *Victoria and Albert II* brought over to Britain many guests for the wedding of Princess Beatrice to Prince Henry of Battenberg – only 11 years later his remains (he died in West Africa) were received on board the *Alberta* and brought to Cowes.

In this chronicle of sea voyages by the British royal yachts, 1886 was the year of the great review of the fleet at Spithead. In the following year, the Queen's Golden Jubilee year, she received a portrait of the royal yacht *Victoria and Albert II* by Admiral Beechey, from the Captain and crew, as a mark of their affection.

This was the time of the great imperial expansion which would end a decade later with the South African war. Great Britain was riding a tidal wave of economic and political success – the most spectacularly successful nation the world had ever seen. Alive with invention, saturated with a generally justified pride over the 50 triumphant years of Queen Victoria's reign, in which the nation had itself reached its own apotheosis in trading terms, the royal yachts represented the gilded figureheads on the ships of state. Between Victoria's Golden and Diamond Jubilees, Britain achieved a record which it can be confidently stated will never be beaten. Around 1891, the British merchant fleet, scattered across the entire globe, carried over 60 per cent of the world's cargoes. They carried 90 per cent of the cargoes between parts of the empire, two-thirds between the empire and the rest of the world, and a third of the rest. British merchant ships carried virtually all the cargoes to and from the United States as well as a good deal of its coastal trade outside the Great Lakes.

All this was backed by a huge navy. When the Queen sailed in the *Victoria and Albert II* between the lines of her battleships at her Diamond Review in 1897, she saw 21 battleships and 54 cruisers among hundreds of other warships. And this was just the home-waters fleet. The two-nation standard meant that British admirals planned that the Royal Navy had to be larger than the next two European navies – at this time France and Germany. Here was an arms race already up and running, and, given the fragility of the European alliances and the depth of the antagonisms (Germany had defeated France just 27 years earlier), it was a recipe for war. In all this, the royal yacht races of the 1880s and 1890s might have looked a foolish adjunct to real power struggles; they were not, especially that running between Britain and Germany. In Kaiser Wilhelm II, with his personal vanity and envy of all things British, there existed a seed which would turn from envy to hate. Although the Kaiser could not start a war on his own account, his influence was formidable.

Royal yachts had, by the end of the nineteenth century, begun to represent in miniature the rivalries of the then great powers, although the French, newly a republic, turned their backs on this vainglorious sideshow. The British, secure in their island fortress, could laugh (and they did) at the pretensions of others, although they succumbed eventually in deciding to replace the *Victoria and Albert II* – against the Queen's wishes. For other monarchs, or presidents of the United States, having some form of official yacht went with the office. The standard set by Queen Victoria and her family might have been unmatchable (except by little Willy) but everyone wanted to be in on this stage somewhere. British shipyards and British designers set the pace, notably GL Watson and Fairfields of Glasgow, but there were many yards and many builders who contributed.

I
f the British were basking in the glories of their self-created Victorian age, across the Channel other nations had long been determined to emulate them – or surpass their successes. Out of the iron will of Bismarck, and the Prussian military code, along with a national desire for improvement, the modern German state was forged in the mid part of the century. After the defeat and humiliation of France by the Germans in 1870, there was no doubt left that Germany would be a force to be reckoned with. The German Empire had been declared on the back of that Franco-Prussian war, and the young Wilhelm II was crowned Kaiser. It was his love of the sea, and his extraordinary mixture of love and envy of all things British, as much as anything, which ensured that Germany would become a major player on the oceans of the world, in a game that lasted at least until 1945.

The Kaiser looked across the North Sea and watched the British Navy; watched, too, his uncle Prince Edward, as he desported himself with a succession of sailing yachts. The rivalry between these two men, which took place in the summer sunlit waters of the Solent, became so intense that it led the Prince of Wales to abandon his most famous yacht *Britannia* (see chapter 7). It also led to the building of bigger and bigger German royal yachts.

The very first on record was the little *Grille*, built by Normands in Le Havre, then a small port on the Normandy coast, in 1857. She was 185 feet long, with a beam of 24 feet and a draught of nine feet. With a top speed of 13 knots, she was powered by a single-expansion steam engine driving a single screw. Little is known about her but she was used in the waters of the Baltic and is thought to have been wooden hulled with three masts. She looked more like a warship than a yacht. In 1914 she became a cadet training ship; she was scrapped in 1920.

Top right The *Hohenzollern* at Cowes in 1899. Kaiser Wilhelm II used her each year as the base from which to launch his annual attack on rival yachtsmen.

Above Kaiser Wilhelm II and his suite aboard the *Hohenzollern* in 1893.

Left The *Kaiseradler* at Cowes in 1892; the *Hohenzollern* was her early 1890s replacement.

The Kaisers also had use of a twin-screw yacht, the *Lorelei*, length about 90 feet, built at Stettin in the Baltic, about which even less is known than the *Grille*.

The second German royal yacht, *Kaiseradler*, was built in Kiel in 1875, and was altogether a different affair. With an overall length of 268 feet, a beam of 34 feet and a draught of 14 feet, she was still relatively modest. Built of iron and rigged with two masts, her engines were oscillating two-cylinder steam paddle wheels. She could reach 15 knots. *Kaiseradler* came at the end of the paddle steamer era, and she represented a fashion rather than a practical aspect of royal and other yachts of her time. As part of her decoration she had shuttered gunport scuttles; inside she exhibited a strict Prussian style, very macho, very *altdeutsch*. Her bell-mouthed funnels lent her a formal, teutonic air, repeated in the much larger *Hohenzollern* which came after.

The *Hohenzollern* was the pride and joy of the German royal family, and, for a while, the biggest royal yacht afloat. She was built by the Vulcan Shipbuilding Company in Stettin in 1893, to a German admiralty design. Overall her length was 383 feet, she had a beam of 46 feet and a draught of 23 feet. She was built of steel, painted white and rigged with three masts. Her Thames tonnage was 3,773, her engines twin triple-expansion steam out of eight Scotch boilers, producing 9,500 hp and a top speed of 21.5 knots. She was expensive enough for objections to be raised in the generally supine German parliament, the Reichstag, where the Government suggested she could be used as a despatch vessel in time of war, as a means of dispelling the row.

Kaiser Wilhelm II now had a yacht he could arrive in at Cowes each August, which would be the envy of his royal relatives and peers. Once

again, the German shipbuilders had produced more of a warship than a pleasure craft – like her ram bow. The imperial double-eagle crest and her gingerbread seem out of place, set against Teutonic might.

One account of the time points out that, while not protected by armour, she did carry eight quick-firing Krupp guns, which were painted white to prevent the ship looking too much like a warship. The decks were laid with linoleum, and when she was in port an awning covered a large part of the deck for lunch or tea parties. Forward there was an extra bridge just for the Kaiser, with access via a mahogany staircase. The Kaiser's apartments were amidships and on the port side. Those of the Empress were on the starboard side. There was a 'very cosy' smoking room fitted out in maple and upholstered in imitation tapestries. The Kaiser's study even had a telephone. The whole ship was fitted with electric lights, then still a novelty at sea.

The dining saloon, on an upper deck, could be made more intimate or enlarged: at 25 feet in width but with a maximum length of 75 feet, it must have been a truly awesome place to eat. When *Hohenzollern* was at Cowes in 1893, in the centre of the dining table was the Queen's Cup, recently won by the Kaiser's yacht *Meteor* at the Royal Yacht Squadron regatta. The family saloon was decorated in blue and silver, with maple fittings, and there was a piano and a porcelain-and-nickel fireplace. English visitors to the *Hohenzollern* were struck by one other feature:

Left The *Hohenzollern* seen at a review of the German fleet.

there were bathrooms attached more or less to every cabin, something they found extremely strange. Elsewhere on the ship was a conference room and a sitting room with chintz upholstery and many hanging photographs of the Kaiser and his family. Everywhere there were paintings, many of them recent, showing the growth of Germany as a nation state and her naval victories. The *Illustrated London News*, remarking on the ship and her owners, reports: 'The Emperor's hearty

Below inset The Kaiser was hit in the face by falling rigging while touring the Norwegian fjords in *Hohenzollern* in 1897.

On board *Hohenzollern* in 1893:
Right The dining saloon.
Below left The drawing room.
Below right The Kaiser's study.

predeliction for seafaring pursuits and recreations, as well as his zeal for the improvement of the German Navy, cannot fail to win the approval of Englishmen. It has been remarked in *The Times*, commenting on the brilliant success of the Cowes Regatta week, that "his Majesty is partly to be thanked for this consummation, British yacht-building has received an immense impetus from the spirit which the Emperor has thrown into the sport... It is a happy circumstance that the Emperor should have taken so keenly to a sport which brings him so frequently among us on terms of intimacy".'

The thoughts ran on – if only the Kaiser could be Anglicised by their common love of the sea, then perhaps the worst fears of the British – exemplified by the scramble for parts of Africa by Germany, France and the British themselves – would go unrealised. It was a hope that lasted, despite the arms races of the first decade of the twentieth century, for another 20 years.

The Great Powers in Europe in the 1890s were Britain, pre-eminently, France, Germany and Russia. The French, however, were only just recovering from their defeat by the Germans in 1870. The Germans were triumphant in all regards on the continent, not least in their burgeoning industrial might. The Russians were in long-term decline, as centuries of feudal neglect worked against reform – particularly of the economy. Nonetheless the Russian royal family did not neglect their pleasures. Before the 1880s the *Standart* was their principal yacht. She was a paddle steamer of 1,100 tons. Her engines could produce 450 hp giving her a speed of 13 knots. She had been built at Bordeaux. The private cabins of the Tsar and Tsarina faced each other, the former fitted with ebony and dark red morocco (goat-skin leather), while the boudoir and sleeping cabin of the Tsarina was quilted throughout with blue satin. There was a splendid semi-circular drawing room aft, and considerable accommodation for the royal household. As for the crew, one account of this ship, while praising the forward accommodation for the ship's officers, says: 'but the men are badly berthed in the orlop without light or ventilation'.

This was in fact true of most royal yachts, for although the accommodation for the ratings on the British royal yachts was better than this, it still meant hundreds of men being crowded into a tiny space for eating, sleeping, washing and toiletries. The Tsars, who, for example, spoke French amongst themselves not Russian, might have been expected to treat their crew worst of all. Even contemporary Western Europe knew things were bad to the East.

It was, no doubt, further concern for their comfort which led the Russian royals to commission the most unusual royal yacht ever built. All the royals suffered from seasickness, some much worse than others. (Queen Victoria admitted it with a kind of stoic pride.) In a general attempt to overcome this problem, for sea voyagers everywhere, the British inventor Henry Bessemer, most famous for the steel-making process which carries his name, thought up an unusual design – for a

Above right An engraving of the Russian yacht *Livadia* in 1881, the most unusual royal yacht ever built.

Below right Four views of the interior of the *Livadia*.

circular ship. The *Livadia*, the Russian royal yacht built on this principle, was commissioned by Tsar Alexander II after an earlier ship of the name had been wrecked in the Black Sea. Built by John Elder and Co, of Govan, near Glasgow, on the Clyde, her design was settled after taking the Bessemer idea and subjecting it to various trials worked on by a Dutch marine engineer, Dr Tideman, and approved by the Russian Admiral Popov. The hull of the *Livadia* was something between an oval and a rhomboid – unkind souls suggested she looked like a turbot. She was built of steel with 48 watertight compartments. At her widest she was 153 feet; her length was 235 feet. She had a pointed bow and an 'obtusely' pointed stern. In the centre she drew 18 feet but her waterline was only six feet above this. At her stern, there was a depression to give the three screws water to drive in. There was no freeboard, the stability given by her immense breadth and by her weight (a staggering 7,700 tons). There were three keels; her bottom had a total area of 14,500 square feet. In the lower hull structure she carried machinery coals and stores. She was said to be capable of 14 knots.

The superstructure contained all the accommodation for the 260 officers and crew in the lower part. Above were the royal apartments. All around the upper works ran a continuous gallery used for stowing anchors, mooring bitts, boat hoists, steam launches and a steam yacht. What can only be described as a floating palace rose 40 feet above the water. It is said that the royal apartments on this ship would have done credit to lesser palaces ashore. In the reception room, with its 12-foot ceiling, was a fountain surrounded by a bed of flowers. It looked, apparently, like the rooms of Louis XVI's palace at Fontainebleu.

The *Livadia* sailed off to the Black Sea in 1881; her fate is not known. What we do know is that, although she may not have caused

Below The *Standart*, dressed overall, making one of her many appearances at Cowes. The three masts were especially designed for ostentatious flag-flying.

seasickness, while crossing the Bay of Biscay she slammed so badly she had to be put into dry dock at Sevastopol in the Crimea for repairs. Tsar Alexander was assassinated in 1881, so it is unlikely he ever saw her. One account has her lying at Odessa for decades, unused and unloved, until she was sold for scrap in 1920.

More conventionally, the Tsars later built a larger *Standart*, the last of the Russian royal yachts. Commissioned in 1895 she in turn became the world's largest royal yacht until the third *Victoria and Albert* of 1900. She was laid down by Burmeister and Wain in Copenhagen. With a length of 450 feet, a beam of 50 feet and drawing 20 feet, her Thames tonnage was given as 4,334. She had two triple-expansion steam engines fed through 24 Scotch boilers producing a top speed of 18 knots. This grandest of all Russian royal yachts had state rooms and saloons, a chapel and children's rooms. The upper deck was so arranged that the imperial family could use almost its entire length for promenades, games and informal meals, and they came to regard this ship as a refuge from the increasing problems they faced ashore. It was in the *Standart* that Tsar Nicholas reviewed the British fleet at Cowes. After the Revolution in 1917, the *Standart* survived to become the Soviet minelayer, *Marti*. She remained on the Soviet Navy Lists until the mid 1960s.

While the royal families of the Great Powers studied each other's yachts at gatherings such at Cowes, so did the minor royals of Europe and beyond. By the end of Victoria's reign the list of royal yachts across Europe was growing all the time. Even in republican America, presidents were getting in on the act.

The Italian royals had the *Trinacria*, the Spanish the *Giralda*, and the Portuguese the *Amelia* series of yachts. In Holland the Dutch royal

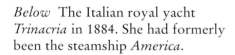

Below The Italian royal yacht *Trinacria* in 1884. She had formerly been the steamship *America*.

Above left The Spanish royal yacht *Giralda* in 1905, a classic Victorian steam yacht and one of the first of this kind to exceed 1,000 tons (Thames Measurement).

Below left The *Dannebrog*, the Danish royal yacht carrying the King and Queen of Denmark in 1914.

Below The *Banshee*, which became the *Amelia III*, the Portuguese royal yacht that finally took the royal family into exile in 1910.

family had *De Valk*, and the Belgian King had the *Alberta*. Further north the Danes had *Dannebrog*, the Swedes *Drott*. To the south the Monagasgue citizens could gaze on *Princess Alice* in the harbour of Monaco, latest in a line of royal yachts built for the principality. Even the Argentine presidents had the *Presidente Sarmiento* to cruise the River Plate and the immense coastline of Argentina.

The *Trinacria* had formerly been the British steamship *America*. Bought by the Italian Government she was refitted with a bowsprit and figurehead. The Spanish yacht *Giralda* had previously been owned by an American, Colonel Harry MacCalmont. Designed and built by Cox, King and Fairfield in 1894, she was a steel twin-screw schooner-rigged ship, with a Thames tonnage of 1,506. Overall her length was 306 feet, and she had a beam of 35 feet, drawing 18 feet. Originally the Spanish Navy had used her as a despatch boat, but then she was fitted out as the royal yacht after the accession of Alphonso XIII in 1902. Nothing is known of her after 1935, just before the start of the Spanish Civil War after the monarchy had fallen.

Many monarchies were to fall just before and after the First World War, including the Portuguese royal family. Their last royal yacht, *Amelia III*, took them into exile. Named *Banshee* when she was owned by Colonel MacCalmont she was then sold to the Portuguese Government. She had been built by Ramage and Ferguson at Leith in 1900. With a length of 229 feet, a beam of 29 feet and drawing 11 feet, she was also steel hulled and schooner rigged. Her Thames tonnage was recorded as 900. King Carlos was assassinated in 1908, and in 1910 the *Amelia III* steamed into Gibraltar harbour carrying into exile the rest of

his family. After this she was renamed again, this time *Cinco du Octuobro*, and taken up by the Portuguese Navy as a despatch vessel. In 1936 she was altered to become a gunboat, fitted with two 47mm guns. Her fate after this time is unknown.

Princess Alice replaced the 200-ton schooner *Hirondelle* as the Monagasgue royal yacht in 1891. She had been built by R and H Green of London with a composite hull of steel frames. She was rigged as a three-masted topsail schooner. In length 180 feet, with a beam of 27 feet and a draught of 12 feet, her Thames tonnage was 593. She had a single screw driven by a simple expansion three-cylinder engine. Prince Albert of Monaco used her as he had used his earlier yachts – for marine and oceanographic research. A world authority, he ranged from the Tropics to the Arctic. Because of this, *Princess Alice* was a sturdy ocean-going ship with a stove-pipe funnel just in front of the mizen mast. Her engine was used as auxiliary power only.

Severely practical uses for royal yachts were unusual: most were on call for state occasions or for the pleasures of getting away from it all. Some royals used their yachts purely for pleasure. The King of the Belgians, Leopold II, who ruled from 1865 to 1909, and who amassed a huge personal fortune, kept *Alberta*, his royal yacht, at Cap Ferrat in the South of France for much of the year. He helped create the town as a fashionable resort. At the end of each day, he'd go ashore, be helped onto a motortricycle, and put off into the sunset to entertain his mistress Caroline Lacroix.

Alberta had begun life as yet another American-owned yacht, the *Margarita*, built for the American millionaire AJ Drexel. Laid down by Ailsa Shipbuilding of Troon, from designs by the doyen of steam yacht design GL Watson, she was 257 feet long, had a beam of 34 feet and drew 15 feet. Another steel-hulled schooner-rigged vessel (the choice for the rich American businessmen who were building steam yachts at an astonishing rate), she could make 17 knots out of her two quadruple-expansion eight-cylinder steam engines producing 448 hp. After King Leopold II's death she was reputed to have been used by the Russian Navy in 1918, and then by the Royal Navy as *HMS Surprise* in the Second World War.

AJ Drexel turns up in another part of this story. The Archduke Charles Stephen of the Austro-Hungarian dual monarchy, had Ramage and Ferguson build for him the *Ul* (meaning beehive). Her name was said to be what the Archduke thought of his extensive and noisy family. Laid down in 1911, she was 187 feet long, with a beam of 29 feet and a draught of 16 feet. Once again steel hulled with two masts and a Thames tonnage of 709, she had well-fitted accommodation on two decks. She was handed over to Italy at the end of the First World War as part of the reparations, along with the *Miramar*, another Austro-Hungarian royal yacht. Through the intervention of the King of Spain she was handed back to her owner who later sold her to AJ Drexel. He renamed her *Sayonara*.

The rest of the world of princes and kings had, as we have seen, taken a firm interest in the development of royal yachts and had ordered their own when the opportunity arose. The Kings of Siam in particular seemed anxious to keep up with their European counterparts. Nearby, in Burma, the King had a 1,000-ton ship built, the *Tsekya Yeen Byan* (Flying Scud), by Palmers on the Tyne, in 1871. She was sent through the Suez Canal, the first steamer that left London direct for Rangoon. Over 200 feet long, with a beam of 26 feet, and drawing 18 feet, she had compound steam engines capable of giving 600 hp, and she made 13 knots on her trials. She made at least one return journey to London, bringing back the Burmese Ambassador.

A few years later the King of Siam ordered an iron-hulled schooner, the *Vesatri,* from Messrs Day, Summers and Co of Southampton. She was fitted with a hoisting propeller and a Whitworth gun in the bows. Below decks she had a dining saloon and a sleeping cabin for the King, as well as a boudoir for his wives. There was separate accommodation for the Captain, the engineering officer and a surgeon – unusual for its time. She had a length of 144 feet, a beam of 22 feet, and a maximum draft aft of 11 feet, weighing in at 280 tons. In 1897, a later King of Siam arrived at Spithead in another royal yacht, *Maha Chakri*, to visit the elderly Queen Victoria. Very little is known of this yacht although she was an impressive sight.

Below inset The King of Siam is greeted by the Duke of York at Spithead in 1897.

Below The King of Siam's yacht, the *Maha Chakri,* anchored in the Solent in 1897.

Top The *Safa El Bahr* in 1900. She was often to be seen in the Sea of Marmaris.

Above The *Mahroussa*, still afloat today. Here she is in her second manifestation – the original length, but with her paddle wheels replaced by screws.

If the Kings of Siam were indulging themselves in ever more opulent yachts, so were the various rulers of the Levant, which was by the end of the century tottering on its last legs. In 1894 the *Safa El Bahr* had been built by Inglis of Glasgow for the Khedive of Egypt, Abbas II, to join the *Mahroussa*. She was used a good deal to cruise in the Sea of Marmaris. Over 200 feet in length, with a beam of 27 feet, and drawing 12 feet, she was highly decorated inside and out, reflecting a style in Middle Eastern yachts that has continued to the present day.

The Turks, on the other side of the eastern Mediterranean, had continued to build and use various yachts. In 1898, the *Teshrifiyeh*, a single-screw vessel of 78 tons, was in use by Sultan Abdul Hamid; in 1903 there was, additionally, the screw barge *Seughudlu* and, finally, in 1903, the *Erthogroul*. The *Erthogroul* was built by Armstrong Whitworth in Newcastle-upon-Tyne for Mohammed V who was, in effect, the last of the Ottoman emperors. She was 264 feet in length, with a beam of 28 feet and she drew 14 feet. Powered by two triple-expansion six-cylinder steam engines, driving twin screws, she was an impressive sight, not least because of a large deckhouse abaft the mizen on the shelter deck. With its close-fitting awning, this was the harem.

If the Ottomans were indulging themselves in an orgy of ships built for their private pleasures, on the other side of the world the burgeoning United States and her succession of presidents had kept strictly to business. The very first presidential 'yacht' had been the *River Queen*, a 556-ton steamer rented for use by President Lincoln at $241 a day – a high price much influenced by the Civil War. She made a number of short cruises on the Potomac, and on 3rd February 1865 she was the venue for a meeting between Lincoln and the Confederate War Commissioners which paved the way for the ending of the Civil War.

The first proper presidential yacht, however, was the *Despatch,* a screw brigantine of 560 tons, 174 feet long, with a beam of 26 feet, and drawing 12 feet. She set a precedent in that for many years presidential yachts were owned and maintained by the US Navy and doubled as naval vessels – in the strict sense that they were used on naval duties when not needed for civil purposes. The *Despatch* was in use by the US Navy between 1873 and 1880, but between 1880 and 1890 she made a number of cruises on the Potomac with President Hayes. After 18 years of service she was wrecked on the Virginian coast.

She was replaced by the *Dolphin*, with a tonnage of 1,465, built by John Roach of Pennsylvania in 1884. In length 240 feet, with a beam of 32 feet and a mean draught of 14 feet, she was a three-masted screw

Below The American despatch-vessel *Dolphin* in 1891. She was used by President McKinley.

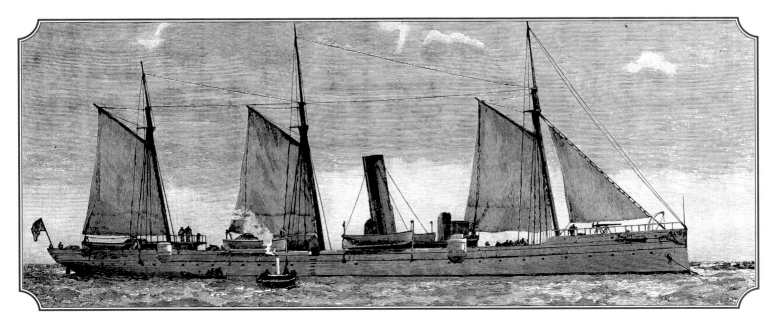

Above The American vessel *Mayflower* can be said to be the first yacht fit for presidential purposes. President Theodore Roosevelt stayed aboard her during the peace negotiations which ended the Russo-Japanese War in 1905.

steamer. As with her predecessor, she was a navy vessel first and foremost, but she was used in a presidential role on a number of occasions. In 1897, for example, President McKinley was aboard her for ceremonies at Grant's Tomb, and he made cruises in her during 1900 and 1902. She had a ram bow, a slightly set-back stem and an overhanging stern, a reminder of the poop decks of old sailing ships. Her masts were heavily raked. Much smaller, but in commission at the same time, was the *Sylph*, a steam yacht of 152 tons, in length 123 feet and with a beam of 20 feet. She had been bought for $50,000 and used by President Theodore Roosevelt, usually at his summer house at Oyster Bay. She had a clipper bow and a counter stern – every inch the steam yacht.

The first yacht for use by presidents that might be said to be truly fit for the purpose was the *Mayflower*. She had been built on the Clyde to a design by GL Watson for American millionaire Ogden Goelet. She was 275 feet long, had a beam of 36 feet and drew 17 feet. Powered by twin triple-expansion steam engines, she could produce 2,400 hp and attain 16.5 knots. Her Thames tonnage was 1,806. She took part in the blockade of Cuba during the Spanish-American war, but in 1902 she was assigned to be the official US state yacht. During the peace negotiations between Japan and Russia in 1905 President Theodore Roosevelt used her as the conference centre.

The *Mayflower* stayed in use as a presidential yacht for the administrations of Taft, Harding and Coolidge, but when Hoover came to power he ordered her to be laid up in the interests of economy. Sadly she was engulfed by fire in 1931, withdrawn from the Navy List and sold, to be used one more time as a coastguard cutter by the Americans in the Second World War. She was sold privately in 1947. Renamed *Mala* she was used to take Jewish refugees from France to Israel.

If the *Victoria and Albert II* represented the royal yacht most associated with the Victorian age, her replacement, the third *Victoria and Albert* probably represented the apogee of all royal steam yachts. She was never used by the old Queen who had resisted to the last any idea that the *Victoria and Albert II* should be paid off, just as she had resisted the idea that there should be electric lights on her. On her death it was the much smaller yacht, *Alberta*, that took her from the Isle of Wight back to the mainland, the *Victoria and Albert II* following in her wake with the new King, Edward VII, on board. After that short voyage the *Victoria and Albert II* never sailed with royalty aboard again. Shortly after the Queen was buried her great yacht was dismantled and laid up. Although Edward VII had wanted her for his Coronation Naval Review it was decided it would be too expensive to refit her even if it could have been done in time.

The last of the *Victoria and Albert* series of royal yachts had, like her predecessors, been built at Pembroke Dock. She had been designed by Sir William White, director of naval construction, as a steel vessel, covered with teak planking and copper-bottomed.

Inset below The body of Queen Victoria being received aboard the *Alberta* at Cowes in 1901.

Below The *Alberta* entering Portsmouth Harbour with Queen Victoria's body on board.

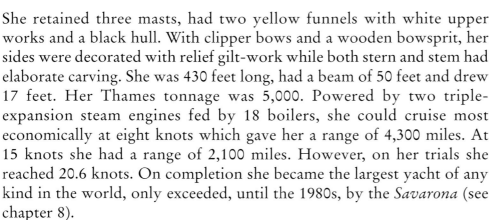

She retained three masts, had two yellow funnels with white upper works and a black hull. With clipper bows and a wooden bowsprit, her sides were decorated with relief gilt-work while both stern and stem had elaborate carving. She was 430 feet long, had a beam of 50 feet and drew 17 feet. Her Thames tonnage was 5,000. Powered by two triple-expansion steam engines fed by 18 boilers, she could cruise most economically at eight knots which gave her a range of 4,300 miles. At 15 knots she had a range of 2,100 miles. However, on her trials she reached 20.6 knots. On completion she became the largest yacht of any kind in the world, only exceeded, until the 1980s, by the *Savarona* (see chapter 8).

She had been laid down in 1897, but her launch was delayed by an accident that occurred while she was in dry dock to receive her machinery. Because so many alterations had been made to the fittings above the waterline during her building she had become wildly top heavy, and on the day she was undocking she began to list until she was

Above left Edward VII aboard his sailing yacht *Britannia* in conversation with Alfonso XIII of Spain.

Above right The last *Victoria and Albert* sailing off Pantelleria in the Mediterranean with Edward VII.

nearly broadsides over, only holding off the water by her mooring lines. For some time there was a question over whether she would ever be used as a royal yacht. After a number of calculations and an enquiry, a good deal of the 'top hamper' was taken off. It was for this reason, apart from sentiment, that caused Queen Victoria never to go on board. She saw the new *Victoria and Albert* only once, from the shore, when the ship was on passage to Portsmouth. The cost of taking off the top hamper was huge – £46,000 – nearly 10 per cent of her original cost.

The last *Victoria and Albert* was a richly furnished and well-appointed ship, in use from 1901 until the outbreak of the Second World War. She was finally broken up in 1954. She took a number of items from earlier royal yachts – her hand-steering wheels and binnacles, for instance, came from the *Royal George*. On her bulwarks, aft, were mounted four old, ornamental brass swivel-guns, two on each side. These three-and-a-half-foot weapons, from 1734, were elaborately embossed with royal arms. They had been on board

the *Royal George* as well. The new *Victoria and Albert* also had two six-pounder bronze muzzle-loaders from the *Victoria and Albert II*.

The accommodation for the royal family was as opulent as might be expected. But the *Victoria and Albert* had a complement of 367 officers and men as well as 40 royal servants. All these had to be accommodated, the crew crammed into the fo'c'sle on the main, lower and orlop decks (not dissimilar to that of the Russian royal yachts). An examination of the ship's plans shows just how crowded this space would have been for the men whose deck space for recreation was also very limited. The officers enjoyed slightly more room, but not much.

The first official voyage of the third *Victoria and Albert* was to take Edward VII to the Dutch port of Flushing. Shortly afterwards she went on a trial cruise to Gibraltar, and in Lisbon she was visited by the King of Portugal. In March 1902, the King and Queen used her for a visit to Dartmouth where they laid the foundation stone of the Dartmouth Naval College. Afterwards, like his mother long before, the King went on to visit the west country and the Scilly Isles. Edward VII had acute appendicitis shortly before his Coronation in 1902, a life-threatening

Top The luxurious interior of the third *Victoria and Albert* showing the royal dining saloon in 1904.

Above Workmen busily engaged in preparing the *Victoria and Albert* for a convalescent trip by King Edward VII in 1925. Portholes are being tested using a powerful water hose.

Right The *Victoria and Albert* in 1897. This was the last ship of her name; she was finally broken up in 1955.

condition which had to be operated on immediately. He recovered, and used the royal yacht as his convalescent home, cruising around the Solent and the Isle of Wight.

At the Coronation Review at Spithead later that year, the royal procession was led, as always, by a Trinity House vessel, in this case the *Irene*, followed by the *Victoria and Albert*, the *Osborne*, the *Alberta* and the Admiralty yachts *Enchantress* and *Firequeen*. Afterwards, the royal family left for a cruise to Scotland.

Throughout King Edward's reign the royal yacht usually went on a Mediterranean cruise in the spring. The destination tended to be either Corfu or Athens, where Queen Alexandra would meet her brother the King of the Hellenes. Summer 'duties' usually ended with the royal yacht taking the Queen to Christiania to see her daughter, the Queen of Norway, and then on to Copenhagen for a visit to her family there.

In 1903 the royal yacht took the King to Lisbon; in 1904 to Germany. In the latter voyage the yacht passed down the Kiel Canal, escorted on shore by detachments of German cavalry on the bank, changed every 12 miles. There was much laughter on board as these hapless riders frequently got bogged down, the horses throwing their stiff-backed riders into the mud.

In 1906 the royal yacht was at Marseilles before travelling on via Sicily to Corfu and then Athens. Later that summer the Prince and Princess of Wales went in her to Norway for the Coronation of King Haakon VII and Queen Maud. The Norwegians had only gained full independence from Sweden in 1905.

Below The royal yacht *Alexandra* was built in 1906, a miniature of the last *Victoria and Albert*. She was sold after the First World War to Norway, where she was used as a pleasure steamer. She was finally sunk by German bombs in 1940.

Above The third *Victoria and Albert* passing *HMS Lord Nelson* in the Solent during the Coronation Review of 1911.

Left George V (right) pictured with Tsar Nicholas II of Russia, in their summer yachting rig.

In 1908 the old royal yacht *Osborne* was sold. Her replacement laid down in 1906 was the *Alexandra*. Built on the Clyde she was a miniature version of the *Victoria and Albert* – a third her size. She was frequently used for cross-Channel service, although she once cruised in Swedish waters. In 1925 she was sold for use as a pleasure steamer in Norway as an economy measure in the austere post-war years.

In 1910 the *Victoria and Albert* took Queen Alexandra on a visit to Athens. She returned overland from Venice, and it was while the yacht was on her way back to England that the King died. With the King's death it is true to say that the great Victorian era at last came to an end, having hung on for a decade into the twentieth century.

The new King, George V, was a sailor through and through. His first use of the *Victoria and Albert* was for the Review of the Fleet in July 1910. He passed through the lines of 36 battleships, 34 cruisers, 48 destroyers, seven submarines and 10 auxiliaries – 135 ships in all, manned by 3,140 officers and 52,000 men. It was another demonstration of the might of the Royal Navy, soon to be tested in the terrible war, by then looming in the background.

For while the British had been basking in the first 10 years of the twentieth century, in a haze of Edwardian decadence, the sun had been slowly sinking for the glory days. On paper still the richest, most civilised, most successful nation on earth, the British were being inexorably challenged. Although they had signed a historic alliance with France after centuries of overt and covert conflict (an alliance joined by Russia shortly after) new nations were pushing themselves aggressively onto the world stage. In the Far East, Japan had taken on and annihilated Russia at sea and on land. In the new world the United States had wiped the floor with a corrupt and collapsing Spain in both the Caribbean and the Philippines. In Europe the Germans were ever sharpening their appetite for war.

One can detect in all this an inter-generational rivalry: Uncle Bertie versus his nephew, Willy, the German Kaiser. As we shall see in chapter 7, some of this rivalry began on the unlikely waters of the Solent. It was undoubtedly there that Willy began to envy British naval might, and took home long-harboured desires to match the British in naval power – which had done so much for the British economy, as well as building up a huge empire.

For whatever reasons, and there were many, the seeds of conflict were germinating. Much was on the international stage; some was in the increasingly deadly alliances being made across Europe that meant small nations in the Balkans would be able to draw in the Great Powers to their internecine and petty disputes. And maybe just a little was in the family rivalries of the European royals with the same kind of squabbles that beset any extended family.

As a footnote to history, that rivalry extended, at the last, overtly to royal yachts because the Kaiser had asked for, and got, what would have

Above At the naval review of 1886 the *Victoria and Albert II* (in the background) receives the royal salute.

been the *Titanic* of all royal yachts. She was never completed because the war had begun, but at 520 feet long and with a projected tonnage of 7,300, she would have dwarfed the *Victoria and Albert*, the *Standart*, and all the rest. She lay unfinished in the Vulcan Stettin yard until she was finally broken up in 1923. By then Germany had entered a new era, and the Kaiser was in exile. But more than that, the world had changed beyond recognition, and millions of young men had lain dead for five years or more, witness to the vanity of men and the foolishness of their dreams.

CHAPTER 6

CUSTOMS AND TRADITIONS

B y the time King Edward VII succeeded Queen Victoria in 1901, and the long hazy days of Edwardian Britain melted into one another (the last sunshine before the deluge of the First World War), the practices and routines of life aboard a royal yacht had become well established. Everything was governed by precedence, that great *modus operandi* of royal households all over the world. On a ship, like ships anywhere, precedence was rooted alongside that of seamanship, for the greater safety of all.

The royal yachts of the time of Edward VII were generally laid up during the winter when repairs and refits could be undertaken. They were in service between April and November. Edward VII had long established for himself an annual trip to the Mediterranean, and these continued while he was on the throne. When the King and Queen arrived they were 'piped' aboard; this custom applied as well whenever they went ashore or if they returned from a shore trip. Usually they were attended by an admiral. The starboard gangway was reserved for their sole use.

On board, the routines of the yacht closely followed those of contemporary warships. Weather reports were taken to the King at 7am and at 9pm. When the yacht was on passage the admiral would take the ship's charts to the King at 10am, and after dinner at night.

The practice on British royal yachts of not shouting or even calling orders had long been a part of the etiquette; it continues on *Britannia* to this day. It was part of the duty of every member of the crew to know what he ought to do; a gesture from an officer was all that was required. For instance, the officer of the watch called boats alongside and had

Detail above Pomp and circumstance: Edward VII every inch a king.

Right King George V and Queen Mary disembarking from the *Victoria and Albert* very carefully indeed.

them hoisted to the davit heads by signs, not shouts. At night the officers and crew crept about in rubber-soled shoes. In an only-just post-Victorian navy, where flogging was still in the punishment details, on the royal yachts the standard punishment was removal from the ship's company, and a return – in disgrace – to general service. Although working conditions on royal yachts were no better, and sometimes worse, than those on warships, the kudos of being a royal yachtsman was sufficient reward.

The Edwardian period represents a moment when pomp and circumstance climbed the twin peaks of flummery and farce. The earlier more relaxed style of the royal yachts of the first years of Queen Victoria was now replaced by rigidity and rules. On the third *Victoria and Albert* the full complement was a flag officer or captain in command; 14 commissioned officers; eight commissioned warrant officers; 122 upper-deck ratings of whom 90 were riggers; 135 engine-room ratings of whom 83 were stokers; 53 Royal Marines; 33 daymen; one civilian stewardess. These 367 officers and crew were accommodated forward. It would be more accurate to say they were crammed, sardine-like, in the spaces forward of the bridge and well below decks.

Left The honeymoon of the Duke and Duchess of Connaught took place on the *Osborne*.

Left inset The third *Victoria and Albert* passing through the Kiel Canal in 1908. Royal yachts abroad had to be careful to keep customs alive and to the letter.

Below The *Victoria and Albert* passing between lines of warships at sea. Every man jack knew his duty.

For the officers, their quarters ran between the state apartments and the fo'c'sle where the men messed. In this space on the main or state deck, cabins ran each side, with corridors – the centre of the ship being taken up with the forward-funnel casing. The fore part, under the bridge, was the wardroom which was as wide as the ship, except for a narrow gangway and some cabins on the port side. The smoking room of the wardroom officers was on the upper deck on the starboard side under the bridge, and some of their cabins were on the lower deck. The admiral had both a day and a sleeping cabin. The desk and the bookcase for him came from the Queen's old dining room and sitting room. The chairs in the wardroom were from the old *Victoria and Albert II* state dining room. With all the officers present 15 sat down to dinner, including the admiral when he was not dining with the royals aft. The wardroom could be divided into two, using a curtain, so half could be instantly turned into a sitting room.

On the bulkheads were pictures and photographs of the royal family. The record of service of every officer who had served in the principal royal yacht was kept in volumes in the wardroom bookcases.

The forward end of the after-funnel casing and the corridors outside the officers' cabins on the state deck were a portrait gallery of former captains. The six original portraits, with dates from 1843 to 1884, came from the Queen's dining room on the old *Victoria and Albert* and had

been painted by Rosa Koberwein in 1877. In 1905 Commodore Colin Keppel found photographs to fill the gaps, and there was then a complete set.

The warrant officers' cabins and mess were on the lower deck on the port side. There was room for seven, all of whom were fully commissioned. For the remainder of the ship's company there was the space forward of the bridge on the main, lower and orlop decks. Also on the orlop deck, aft, was the engineer's stores and the wardroom storeroom. Forward was the boatswain's and shipwright's stores, the sail and flag lockers and the spirit room. There wasn't a lot of room for the 350 or so men and marines to sleep, eat and spend time off duty.

In the 1880s the master-at-arms and a ship's corporal were replaced by a chief boatswain's mate and a petty officer, first class. The change was made because it was felt that as the crew were chosen men of good character, then ship's 'police' were superfluous. However, a ship's fiddler was still carried, a survivor of sailing-ship days when music was supplied for weighing anchor, hoisting sail and general hauling.

The single woman on the naval complement, the stewardess, had been brought in in 1847 to look after the royal apartments. The British Admiralty decreed she should be paid at the same rate as a petty officer, but should not be called one. She was borne on the ship's register, nonetheless and received a ship's book number. In 1881 Mrs Mary Jane Hooper, who held the post, was recommended for a long-service and good-conduct medal by the then Commander of the *Victoria and Albert II*. As there was no precedence for this, the Lords of the Admiralty were unable to approve it. Mary Jane Hooper died – still in service on the royal yacht – the following year.

The royal apartments were in the charge of a keeper and an assistant keeper – which had been the case as long as anyone could remember. Another assistant was added in 1901. These three were, in effect, a

Top The Russian royal yacht *Polar Star* at Reval in June 1908.

Above A programme of entertainments signed by members of the Russian royal family at Reval in June 1908. Every member whose name is signed here was executed by Russian communists in 1918.

steward and two assistant stewards. They had no special uniform until Edward VII suggested it in 1904. Approval was given and the steward got a warrant officer's kit, and the assistants had rating's uniforms, with buttons stamped with a royal cipher surmounted by a royal crown.

Royal yachts had been commanded by captains with long service who gave up their right to promotion as it fell due in favour of the honour of being in charge of a royal ship. A flag officer as commanding officer was only authorised by Order in Council in 1892. When this was first agreed, the flag of the officer concerned was not allowed to be flown, due to the complexity of the rules, and because the Victorian navy – let alone the royal family – was obsessed with doing things 'right'. But in 1903, Rear-Admiral Hedworth Lampton pointed out that 'it was difficult to explain to foreigners the reason for not flying a [ie *his*] flag' and the Admiralty, now no doubt more scared of being laughed at by other navies than of upsetting royal yacht precedence, agreed. The flag could be flown.

This issue had nothing on a previous furore created by royal yachts and their semi-independent practices. Naval ships in the past had fired a morning and an evening gun to set the night watches. This was the precedence of the most senior ship (considered for this purpose the equivalent to an officer). In 1872 the *Victoria and Albert II* was in Portland harbour on the south coast, with the Prince of Wales on board representing the Queen at the annual summer manoeuvres. To the horror of the senior navy men present both the flagship of the Channel Fleet *and* the *Victoria and Albert II* fired the morning and evening guns (the royal yacht's being two six-pounder bronze muzzle loaders). In the consternation that followed it transpired that this practice had been

Below A banquet on board the Russian royal yacht *Standart* at Cowes in 1909. Etiquette, including the wearing of hats, was rigidly enforced. The Tsarina is wearing the highly feathered one, extreme right of the picture.

followed when the Queen had been on board for her trips to Cherbourg and on many other occasions. The view of the officers on the royal yachts was that they were always the senior ship, whatever the circumstance, and whether or not royalty was on board. After 1872 the practice was allowed to continue, but only for the evening gun. Queen Alexandra, when on board, was able to do this by pressing an electric switch at the dinner table, and she delighted in doing so, startling the dinner guests who had not been subject to the very loud bang before, including at least one bishop.

By this time ratings on royal yachts were all volunteers who had to fulfil certain requirements as to character, sea service and physique. They generally remained on the yacht for which they were picked until they retired. Promotion on the yacht came only when a vacancy occurred through someone else's retirement. If a rating or officer wanted promotion he could either elect to stay on the yacht at his current rank and wait, or be promoted out of it. As compensation for this possible loss of promotion, ratings were allowed to serve an extra five years providing they were fit. In some exceptional circumstances they were allowed another five years on top of this, drawing both their pay and their pension.

From late Victorian times onwards, British royal yacht crew had an extensive sport and entertainment programme during the year. There was sailing and rowing, with annual regattas at Cowes, Southampton, Ryde, Southsea, Calshot and Portchester, all Solent ports. There was a water-polo team and a cricket team which had a long list of fixtures at home and away. In the winter there was football. Because it was the Navy there was inevitably a tug-o'-war team.

Social gatherings included an annual summer sports day and Christmas. The on-duty watch on Christmas Day would arrange a party for crew and families. The royal-yacht concert party organised entertainments for the officers and the ship's company on board, and for the wives and relations of yachtsmen in locations ashore. Sometimes the shows on the ship were attended by royalty.

Any painting of a British royal yacht from Victorian times onwards shows three flags flying from the masts when the sovereign is on board. These are the Royal Standard, the Admiralty flag and the Union flag. The Royal Standard is the personal flag of the king or queen and is flown at the mainmast head. The use of this flag can be traced back as far as the twelfth century, but its design has not stayed the same over time. In the past it was also used by

Below The *Victoria and Albert* and the *Standart* receive a salute from assembled warships at Cowes in 1909. The photograph was taken from the deck of the *Standart*.

Inset right A group on board the *Standart* at Cowes in 1909, including George, Prince of Wales (left), King Edward VII (centre) and Tsar Nicholas II of Russia (right).

Below right A group on board the royal yacht *Britannia* in 1921, including King George V, Queen Mary and Princess Mary.
On board the *Standart* and *Britannia*, the formality is what most impresses itself on the modern observer.

admirals as well as sovereigns, and it was used as a signal flag to summon flag officers.

The Admiralty flag developed out of an ornamental flag displaying the badge of the Lord High Admiral. The earliest example of the 'anchor' flag can be seen in an engraving of the *Ark Royal*, Howard of Effingham's flagship, at the Armada in 1588. But this was only of an anchor. The 'foul' anchor – with the cable entwined around it – first appeared in the seventeenth century. From 1964, when the Admiralty dropped Lord High Admiral from its ranks when the Ministry of Defence was formed out of the three previous armed-service ministries, the Queen took on the 'job' (and the flag) for herself.

The Union flag dates from 1606 when it consisted of a combination of the red cross of St George and the white saltire of St Andrew. The red saltire, for St Patrick, was added on the union of England and Scotland with Ireland, in 1801.

The custom of flying all three flags together to mark the presence of the sovereign on board dates from the Restoration in 1660. When the king or queen is not on board but, say, the Prince of Wales is, his own flag will be flown from the mainmast. Similarly, if a foreign king is aboard on his own, his flag will be flown. There were variations on this theme. In 1907, when the King and Queen of Denmark crossed the Channel in the *Victoria and Albert* to review the French fleet, the French ensign was hoisted at the fore,

the Danish standard was at the main, and the white ensign at the mizen. In 1905 the King of Greece, who was an honorary British Admiral, flew both the white ensign and his own standard alongside each other at the mainmast when he crossed from Cherbourg to Portsmouth.

Royal yachts have always been escorted. Requests for these escorts were formally sent to the Admiralty, with the number and class of vessel required and, where possible, for what times. During Cowes Week, for example, a destroyer was in attendance (from late Victorian times) as well as a minesweeper for when the Prince of Wales was racing his yacht *Britannia*. The *Victoria and Albert* had a battleship or two surrounding her. During Edward VII's reign, whenever he went to the Mediterranean for his summer cruises, two cruisers (appropriately) were in attendance if he was on board, but only one was allowed for the Queen. There were usually two to four destroyers as well, used to fetch and carry mail, and the all-important King's messenger. But when the King went to visit Germany in 1904 he had four cruisers and six destroyers, a kind of keeping up with the Joneses in naval terms, as the Kaiser was by then hell-bent on bettering the British at sea come what may.

Being on a royal yacht was not just a matter of highly organised protocols and precedences, setting rules for just about every contingency. Photographs at the turn of the century demonstrate this amply: the faces of everyone, including the royals, are often distorted with what can only be described as a kind of social agony, a constant fear that any minute now someone was going to do something not covered by the book.

Life on, or near, a royal yacht was also very noisy. The regulations said that whenever the royal standard was hoisted or hauled down on the royal yacht, then warships, British and foreign, and shore batteries nearby, all had to fire a royal salute – this was 21 guns. How the good folk of the Solent must have dreaded Cowes Week with all its royal comings and goings. The same salute had to be fired by every passing warship. Queen Victoria, ever a stickler for protocol, decreed in 1874 that while she was at Cowes her guardship was *not* to fire a salute unless it was intended for foreign royalty. No such thoughts ever seemed to have passed through the addled brains of her son, addled partly perhaps from the noise.

The somewhat quieter custom of piping the sovereign aboard is a very old one on British ships, going back at least to Henry VIII in the sixteenth century. On warships in general anyone of commanding rank gets this treatment; on the royal yachts it is only accorded to the sovereign. The pipe is a boatswain's whistle and the piping is done by the boatswain or his mate, sounding for about 12 seconds, beginning on a low note, then rising to a medium note before falling again.

Two other customs are worth noting. The first is a reverse of normal naval practice which is to drink the loyal toast sitting down. This is said to have begun because officers would bang their heads on the low deckheads of old warships, so they were allowed to drink sitting. In the

Above The Queen and Prince Philip aboard *Britannia* with their entourage. Formality remains a keynote with British royals.

royal yachts, however, the loyal toast is drunk standing up.

Whenever a royal yacht leaves port in Britain, it has been the custom for centuries for a Trinity House ship to precede her. This duty, laid on the Elder Brethren of Trinity House, who still look after the buoys and marks around the British and Irish coasts, goes back to the Middle Ages, and it is exercised on every possible occasion. It was the practice for many years to embark a Trinity House pilot onto the royal yacht while at sea round the British coast, although this is no longer the case.

Getting the royals to and from the royal yachts meant using various ships' boats. On the third of the *Victoria and Albert* series there were 13 in all, seven on one side, six on the other. The King had a special motor boat and there was a royal steam barge of 11 tons. There were two steam cutters, one pulling barge, two pulling cutters, one galley, three gigs, two skiffs and, for harbour use when the yacht was in Portsmouth, one steam pinnace, three steam cutters, and eight pulling boats, these latter not carried aboard.

The state barge was manned by petty officers dressed as seamen. The coxswain was the chief boatswain's mate who sat on one 'dickey' seat with a sub-lieutenant on the other. When royalty was in this boat the admiral attended.

Elaborate means were provided and practised to ensure that the transfer of royal persons to and from the shore took place without anything undignified happening. Perhaps the worst nightmare the sailor in charge of one of these small vessels could imagine, if he dared, was the sight of the king or queen falling overboard as he or she tried to get ashore or back onto their royal yacht. As far as is known, this never happened, a testament to the amazing skills of these men and their seamanship.

CHAPTER *7*

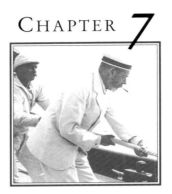

THE GREAT ROYAL
RACING YACHTS
1893–1935

She has been called the most perfect sailing yacht ever built; she served two British kings faithfully for over 40 years; and she won 231 firsts in 635 starts – an unparalleled record. Appropriately, her name was *Britannia,* and she was probably the finest ship ever designed by that doyen of both steam and sailing-yacht designers GL Watson. With her launch in 1893 there came a new era in yacht racing. She was built to skim the waves, rather than plough through them. Where she led others would follow. She cost her new owner, the Prince of Wales, around £8,000, for which he got the complete ship, cabin fittings, sails and all. It was probably the greatest bargain any yachtsman has ever had out of a boatyard. But it ran deeper, far deeper, than mere money.

British first-class yacht racing had reached a low ebb at the end of the summer season of 1892. The root causes can be traced back to the innate conservatism of British yachting, exemplified in the Royal Yacht Squadron, of which 'Bertie' was a member. We will return to the RYS in a moment because its history between the 1860s and the 1930s was to be more intimately connected with royalty and yacht racing than at any time before or since. The conservatism of British yachting in the nineteenth century could be seen in the 'cod's head and mackerel tail' waterplan of the traditional 'English' cutter which carried a great deal of baggy flax canvas aloft. There had been hard racing using these vessels, but it tended to be a courtly affair of wagers and cups – all very Corinthian with more than a tinge of the navy about it. Then, in 1851, came the United States, in the shape of the eponymous schooner *America.*

What happened next has long gone into the mythic realm: it was more shocking to the British at the time than if the young United States

Detail above The Sailor King, George V, lends a hand on board his great racing machine, *Britannia.*

Right George V gave *Britannia* a second lease of life after her first owner, Edward VII, sold her in disgust at the win-at-any-cost attitude of his nephew, the Kaiser.

had invaded the south coast. There had been astonished rumours that the Americans were building a yacht to challenge the fastest in Queen Victoria's realm. When it arrived, and then proceeded to whip the finest the Royal Yacht Squadron could supply into a cocked hat, astonishment gave way to dismay. The RYS cup (now the America's Cup) has never come back, and until the Australians finally managed to get their hands on it for a while, it had been bolted into its mount at the New York Yacht Club, a statement of finality as galling as anything to the British over the past 150 years.

In 1851 Queen Victoria and her party, watching the race from the deck of the *Victoria and Albert* anchored in Alum Bay close to the Needles, were much gratified to see *America* dip her ensign to the royal yacht, while her Captain and crew took off their hats for some minutes. The Queen famously asked rather later in the drawn-out contest who had won. The reply from a signalman has gone into the history books: '*America* first, Your Majesty, there is no second.'

Twelve years later, and one year after the death of his father, the Prince of Wales was unanimously elected a member of the Royal Yacht Squadron. He took up yacht racing with some enthusiasm, though not half as much as his son, George, would. But the Prince of Wales' patronage of yachting, and his visits to Cowes across the bay from Osborne House, were to transform the British (and European) yachting scene, creating in Cowes Week, at the beginning of August, a spectacular part of the English summer 'season'. It was a dazzling opportunity for the aristocracy and the newly rich to mix together in a heady cocktail of socialising and exhilarating sport.

Since the time of King Charles II yacht racing had fallen into desuetude, although by the end of the eighteenth century it had been given a small fillip in the formation of the Royal Thames Yacht Club, originally known as the Cumberland Fleet, in 1775. Yachting was then, and remained for a long time, a very aristocratic business.

The origins of the Royal Yacht Squadron can be found in a meeting of 1st June 1815 when a group of 'nobles and gentlemen', tired of the antics of the Beau Brummel set in London, met at the Thatched House Tavern in St James Street to found a new yacht club. Cowes was already fashionable as a seaside resort on the Isle of Wight: Emma Hamilton had taken a house called Thornhill there, 16 years earlier, ostensibly for sea bathing which was becoming all the rage. The Prince Regent, who became a member of the club in 1817, also had a house on the beach. It was in a letter written from the *Royal George* laying off Brighton to the members then gathered in East Cowes, that he made his request. He was, of course, elected. When he later became King George IV, he gave the club the title 'Royal', so after 1820, it was known for some time as the Royal Yacht Club. Since then, the reigning king has always been Admiral of the Squadron, but Queen Victoria (and Queen

Above 'Twenty Seconds to Go: *White Heather*, *Cambria*, *Alstra*, *Westward*, *Britannia*, *Lulworth*', from a painting by Charles Dixon.

Left George IV helped revive yachting as a serious sport in England, and, in effect, helped to found the yacht club which became the Royal Yacht Squadron.

Elizabeth II) have only been the Patron. The change in name came about because King George IV issued, in 1829, a warrant through the Admiralty allowing members to wear the White Ensign of the Royal Navy when aboard their yachts. Four years after this, because of its perceived services to the Royal Navy through yacht design, the club was granted further permission to be known as the Royal Yacht Squadron, and William IV became its first admiral.

The Royal Yacht Squadron prided itself on how much its members, their yachts and crew, emulated the best the Royal Navy could produce. After Trafalgar – the greatest naval victory the British ever achieved – the Royal Navy went into its own form of self-congratulatory 'naval' gazing. And as the nineteenth century belonged, so everyone concurred, to Great Britain, so the Royal Yacht Squadron grew ever more pompous.

In 1851 hubris stalked the decks of members' yachts. At a fateful committee meeting at the Thatched House, its London HQ, the RYS decided to present a cup for a race open to the yachts of all nations. The course was to be around the Isle of Wight, and the rules were to be set by them. This was the competition Commodore Stevens entered through a syndicate of the New York Yacht Club. The *America*, with her low, black hull and severely raked masts, was a sensation as a design, totally at odds with the other 14 yachts on the start line. Five of these took a wrong turn off the line; the *Arrow* ran ashore, the *Alarm* standing off to assist. Off Ventnor, the leading yachts *Volante* and *Freak* fouled each other. This left *America* to fight it out with *Aurora, Bacchante, Evelyn* and *Brilliant.* By the time she had rounded the Needles and was on her way past the *Victoria and Albert* her lead was immense. In fact *Aurora* caught up and was only eight minutes behind on the finish line, but by then no-one was counting.

The cup that *America* won came to be known as the America's Cup. Once the New York Yacht Club had its hands on the cup, it was determined to hang onto it – by constantly tinkering with the rules for subsequent challenges.

Although British yacht design altered somewhat, it was hampered still by cloying conservatism and by the extremely complex rules surrounding yacht design. It was no consolation that American yachting was suffering too, for the basis of the game from 1851 (whatever was said in public) was to wrest the America's Cup back, and put it where the British firmly believed it belonged: in the glass case at Castle Point.

At the end of the 1892 season, the Earl of Dunraven commissioned GL Watson to design for him a first-class cutter whose sole object was to challenge for the America's Cup. Watson was given a free hand to design this yacht so that she could race in British waters while remaining within the ever-changing rules of the New York Yacht Club. When the Prince of Wales found out about Earl Dunraven's new yacht, the *Valkyrie II,* he ordered his own. Suddenly big yacht racing was alight.

The Prince had owned other yachts: his attention seems to have been fully engaged from 1864 when he watched the racing from the royal yacht tender *Fairy.* He first owned *Dagmar,* named for his sister-in-law and launched in 1866; then *Princess* (1869); *Alexandra* (1871); *Zenobia* (1872); *Hildegarde* (1876); *Formosa* (1880); and *Aline* (1882). But the *Britannia* outshone all of these put together. She was 115 net tons, gross 221 tons. Her length overall was 122-and-a-half feet; on the waterline 89-and-a-half feet. She had a beam of 23 feet seven inches, and drew 16 feet three inches. The original mast was 164 feet from deck to truck. The fittings throughout were of polished yellow pine and mahogany. The interior provided four guest cabins, a spacious saloon, a cabin for the skipper and sleeping accommodation for her full racing crew of 30.

Between 1893 and 1897 she won 147 prizes in 219 races, of which 122 were firsts. In her first racing year she beat *Valkyrie II* and the American cutter, *Navahoe.* It would have seemed as though nothing could stop her progress under her owner's proud eye. Yet, in 1897, he sold her. The reason for this was his nephew, little Willy – Kaiser Wilhelm II of imperial Germany.

Because history is the propaganda of the winners, it's all too easy to demonise those characters in the past whose activities have affected them to their own detriment. As it happens, propaganda in the modern sense of the word, grew out of the often grotesque caricatures of 'the

Right King Edward VII (inset) and his racing yacht *Britannia* under full sail. She was probably the greatest racing yacht ever to be built in a British yard and her grace and beauty inspired a generation of yacht designers. She needed a large crew to sail her flat out.

enemy', whosoever that might be, during the First World War. Kaiser Wilhelm's demonology grew out of all that. But sometimes art imitates life and the last Kaiser does seem to have been an overbearing little man.

He became a member of the Royal Yacht Squadron in 1889, and in 1892 he bought the yacht *Thistle*, renaming her *Meteor*. At least one authority on yachting believes that it was because of this that the Prince of Wales ordered *Britannia*, triggering the violently fought competition which followed, and his own demise. If so, it would be an irony the Kaiser no doubt savoured.

As with the Prince of Wales' enthusiasm for yachting in Britain, the Kaiser's interest in yachting began a craze back in Germany. Prince Henry of Prussia is reputed to have once told a member of the RYS that 'the Germans are not a yachting nation. It is only my brother's interest in yachting that causes our people to go in for the sport. He wishes them to take to yachting and make "Kiel Week" a sort of "Cowes Week" in order to encourage them to take an interest in the navy'.

That interest, Prince Henry went on to say, was to help persuade the Germans that they needed to spend huge sums on their new navy to challenge the Royal Navy sooner or later. Or it was part of the vainglorious attitude of the Kaiser, part of his envy of the British and their Empire, and his desire to match it. Later, during the time of King Edward VII, there were many rumours that the German yachtsmen who flocked to Britain each year were all spies, as Cowes was very conveniently only a couple of miles away from the huge naval base of Portsmouth.

Back in the 1890s, however, the surface of the Solent was being increasingly ruffled as the contest between the Kaiser and the Prince hotted up. The *Thistle,* then *Meteor,* first had an English skipper, although she did carry some German crew. She was replaced by *Meteor II,* larger and with more sail than *Britannia.* It is a curious fact that, despite his egoism and bombast, Wilhelm II was an able sailor who, over the years, trained his crews to the point where, just before the Great War, they were up to the best international standards. The *Meteor* series followed one from another. *Meteor III* was a schooner – the first built in America. By 1909, when German yacht design had caught up, *Meteor IV* was built in Germany, skippered and crewed by Germans. Each time

Above The *Meteor II* in 1899. She was the Kaiser's second instrument in his hard-fought efforts to beat *Britannia.*

Far left above The first in the *Meteor* series. Formerly Thistle, she was the Kaiser's first racing yacht.

Inset The Kaiser overseeing his crew. Spot the difference between him and George V on page 123.

Left All hands on bowsprit. The *Meteor II* aground, with her crew trying to lift her deep keel off the mud.

a new *Meteor* was commissioned the Kaiser turned over the old to a member of his family.

The souring of relations between Bertie and Willy would probably have happened whatever sport they had elected to compete in. Yachting, perhaps, is a sport designed for simmering loathings to boil over not least because of the opportunities to protest at another's conduct at sea through the complex application of racing rules, and the further opportunity to rub in this victory or that defeat in the yacht club later. The Royal Yacht Squadron, with its overly stiff attitudes, lent another dimension: the social rebuff.

It was here, as much as anywhere, that the tension between these two men was palpable. For while the RYS might have huffed and puffed to keep out the large numbers of the newly rich (their wealth accrued from manufacturing, trade or commerce), they needed the continual fresh input of members and their money. Thus it was that, despite continuous attempts to use blackballing when members were proposed, they could not all be kept

Top left The *Meteor III*, schooner rigged and American built.

Left inset Kaiser Wilhelm II in 1908: a man in whom vanity shone like a beacon.

Above *Meteor IV* in 1912, the only German-built yacht of the *Meteor* series.

out. Even if they were, they still turned up in their pretty steam yachts, dropped anchor off the Squadron at Castle Point, and entertained royally – as well as royalty.

The Kaiser watching all this was appalled. For though he longed to recreate that archetypal English casual garden-party atmosphere across the North Sea, he could never get to the bottom of it, so busy was he looking down his nose. He berated Bertie for taking part in antics which he considered well beneath his dignity, such as the time two of the Prince's racier lady friends dressed a live donkey in a nightdress and placed it in Bertie's bed. And he could scarcely believe it when told that Bertie had gone sailing with Thomas Lipton, blackballed from the RYS for being 'a common grocer', although one of the richest men in the land. The Kiel Regatta, over which he presided, was a stiffly Prussian affair, with marching military bands, official dinners and gold braid in every corner. Grocers were definitely not permitted.

So it was that the Prince of Wales, finally losing patience with his nephew's nagging ways which turned Cowes Week, as he put it, into a vexation instead of a relaxation, sold *Britannia* to private owners. It shows the pain of this decision that a mere two seasons later he bought her back; but his heart was not in it. In 1898 she had six starts and took no prizes. In 1900 she was sold for a second time to Sir Richard Williams Bulkelely of Anglesey, and a member of the RYS, who kept her until 1902 when the by-now King Edward VII bought her back a second time, using her only for cruising. Intriguingly, this sale was never registered, the error not being discovered until 1911 when she was transferred to King George V. With his ownership *Britannia* entered a new a glorious career, for King George V was not known as the Sailor King for nothing.

Above Nicholas II, the last Tsar of all Russia, going ashore during the Cowes Regatta of 1909.

The Edwardian era was a short one, a mere decade. It signalled an end not a beginning, although few could have realised it at the time. The end it represented was of that great Victorian period; and as the twentieth century grew weary with wars we would all lament that loss. In the last year of King Edward's reign Cowes had perhaps the greatest gathering of classic Victorian steam yachts and old, great racing yachts that it had ever had. The water was packed with steam yachts, the most outward signs of success, their black or white hulls thick with the gold-leafed gingerbread that was for these ships the same bluff and bluster that their masters wore on their yachting caps.

In this year, 1910, the still relatively new *Victoria and Albert* dominated the scene with her attendant battleships. The *Hohenzollern* was there, as was the *Standart* and the *Giralda*. The King entertained 20 members of the RYS to dinner aboard the royal yacht, and presented them all to the Tsar. With him was King Alphonso XIII of Spain, a keen racing sailor, whose great yacht *Hispania* won many races. King Alphonso rarely missed Cowes Week and he was known for his great sense of fun. Married to one of King Edward's nieces, he could hardly have been further apart in outlook from the Kaiser. Once, arriving at Portsmouth harbour railway station ahead of time, he had leapfrogged over the back of a porter busily engaged in rolling out the red carpet in anticipation of his imminent official appearance.

King George V had a sense of humour, but it was not of this kind. Perhaps in part a reaction to his pleasure-obsessed genial but sometimes vulgar father, he tended to take life much more seriously. He had not expected to become king, his avowed wish being to make a career in the Royal Navy. A disciplinarian as a result, his overwhelming love was of the sea and all its moods. The evidence suggests he was never so happy as when he was on board *Britannia* in a race. He took her tiller, he pulled halliards and lines with his crew, and made merry with them. His language was then more at one with his surroundings, for he could never rid himself entirely of the expletives of naval life.

For the first year of his reign, George V didn't use *Britannia*, and she remained on her mud berth in the Medina River just up from Cowes.

Above George V, a king who, like Charles II, was never more relaxed than at the wheel of his yacht.

Right *Britannia* at Cowes, 1913, painted by N. Sotheby Pitcher.

Below George V keeps a weather eye on his crew as they hoist sail, 1931.

But in both 1912 and 1913 she was raced again – in 23 starts she took 13 first prizes. The great racing yacht was back on form. Then, in August 1914, came the deluge. *Meteor IV* was halfway across the North Sea on her way to Cowes when war was declared and she turned around and went home; *Britannia*, shortly, was to be laid up for six long years, two more than the war lasted.

Meteor IV had been coming from Kiel, which never did match Cowes, although the Kaiser had tried so hard. Just before the war it managed to attract a wide range of yachts and their crews, but all around were the long lines of German warships, and, more sinister, flotillas of submarines. There might, too, have been a huge Zeppelin sliding across the sky, and visiting yachtsmen must have pondered on what it all meant. In the midst of all this the *Hohenzollern* would have been at anchor, her master busy, day by day, with his racing, and no doubt brooding over the shape of things to come. His plans included a mighty replacement for *Hohenzollern* – a ship designed to outclass any royal yacht afloat.

The Great War swept all that away and changed the world forever. The United States, for one, entered the world stage, reluctantly, tentatively, and found herself forced, in the end, to stay. On the far side of the world Japan found herself an ally of the British and the French, and found, too, an opportunity for wild economic expansion.

Yachting took an enforced holiday while its young crews marched back and forth in Europe, and died in the muddy fields of Flanders. The flippancy of the pre-war years would haunt the survivors, as would their very existence. At the end of it all the Kaiser, a much changed man, went into exile and the conflict was put on hold while the protagonists regrouped.

It was not until 1920 that *Britannia* was refitted and made ready for the last phase of her career which lasted another 15 years – in 388 starts she won 96 firsts out of a total of 219 prizes. In 1931 the American measurement rule was adopted in Britain, really to give British yacht designers a lever by which they could prise away that long-coveted America's Cup. King George, after some thought, decided to have *Britannia* rerigged to conform to this rule. One result was that in the very last part of her life, she sported a mast 175 feet high, on which she carried a huge Bermudan main. When first this was tried out no-one knew how the old yacht would behave. One of the crew on board the day she set sail described her leaving her berth 'like a scalded cat'. Several believed her mast – or something more vital – would give way: it didn't.

Below *Britannia* leading a magnificent group of 'J' class yachts at Cowes in 1932.

Below inset King George V and other members of the crew hauling lines aboard *Britannia*.

The new class into which she now entered was known as the J class. The King had enquired of his sailing master why this was, and it was explained to him that J stood for the rating under the universal rule. He is said to have replied that 'it should have been "A"'. When asked why, he said: 'well, "A" is for adultery. I'm the only owner, apart from one other, who still has his original wife'.

The Sailor King was able to put up with spartan conditions above and below decks. His wife, Queen Mary, a woman of immense dignity and a quiet, regal presence, was by contrast no lover of the ocean. Rarely could she be persuaded to go sailing – she became nervous when *Britannia* began to heel as the wind was forced into her huge sails.

In the summer of 1923, however, when *Britannia* was racing on the Clyde, 30 years after she had been launched there, the Queen was on board. The weather had moderated when she embarked although it had been generally at gale force. Not long after, the squalls began again, sweeping down from the mountains all around. Halfway round the course the jib-topsail sheet ran clean out of its blocks leaving the sail flying like a kite, and the sheet whipped angrily across the deck, threatening anyone who went near it. Queen Mary had gone below where the noise of this flailing must have been terrifying. When at last all had calmed somewhat on deck, the King sent a hand below to ask after the Queen. When he came back the King asked him what the Queen had said. The man was hot and bothered, and he had to be asked several times before he would answer. 'She said never again, she's damned if she will,' he finally replied. The King roared with laughter; the Queen did not sail on *Britannia* again.

The yacht was getting old and by 1933 her share of the prizes was beginning to fall off. Yet she could still show her old form, as this account from one of the crew on board the yacht in a race in the Babbacombe Regatta suggests. 'By the time we arrived at the starting line the wind had freshened considerably and, shortly before the start we received a signal from *HMS Sutton*, our escort vessel, to say that a gale was predicted. We saw, too, that both *Velsheda* and *Shamrock* were reefing their mainsails in preparation for a blow. However, as time was short and Hugh Paul, in *Astra*, had evidently decided to carry a whole mainsail, Phil Hunloke [*Britannia*'s famous sailing master] chose not to shorten sail.

'Our course was a triangular one of 45 miles – three times round five-mile legs. By the time the starting gun fired, ominous black clouds had rolled up over the cliffs above Babbacombe and the wind had already freshened considerably.

'Soon after we came on a wind, a few seconds ahead of *Shamrock*, Phil was calling for the sheets to be eased as *Britannia* was beginning to wallow. The third leg of the course gave us a reach, with the wind a little for'ard of the beam, into the starting line. Now *Britannia* heeled to a tremendous angle with the water up to the companion deckhouse. Phil, waist deep in water, was having difficulty steering her. Blinded by

driving spray, he shouted to the second mate to give him a hand at the wheel, and called for a lashing to be tied round his waist to keep him from being swept overboard. We were travelling at fourteen knots and under the press of her whole mainsail and in the savage gusts of wind that crashed down from the high cliffs, the old yacht was practically unmanageable. Her entire lee deck was under water and her mainboom, with the sheet eased, but a few inches from the water. In a cloud of flying spray, we tore through the pleasure boats, hollering at them to keep clear of us and leaving them pitching and rolling in our wake. We had to bear up to sail through the line at the end of the first round.

'"She won't bear up!" Phil shouted as he and the second mate forced the wheel over, the pair of them half buried in foam.

Above 'Jockeying for the Start – King George V Sailing *Britannia* in the Big Class Race, Cowes, 1934', by Charles Eddowes Turner.

Inset King George V (right), in wet-weather gear during a yachting trip on board *Britannia*.

'Then, with a crack, the clew of the jib carried away, mercifully easing our sorely pressed ship.

'Now, our nearest rival, *Shamrock*, was minutes astern of us, so, in the gale and rising sea, Phil refrained from taking any chances and did not even set the spinnaker off the wind. Now, too, *Velsheda* and *Astra* had retired from the race; the latter having carried away most of the hanks on her mainsail.

'Soon after we rounded the weather mark more than five minutes ahead of *Shamrock*, which was lying over almost on her beam ends, I saw her mast go over the side with a mighty splash.

'So the old *Britannia* was the only one left in the race.'

She raced on, all on board praying that the committee boat would declare the race over. Eventually it did and the yacht survived to race another day. But these triumphs were becoming few and far between. The end of her racing career came in 1935. In 20 starts she gained not a single prize and plans were laid for her to carry on only as a cruising yacht. Then, in January 1936, King George V died and his son, King Edward VIII acceded to the throne.

The old King had left instructions in his will that if none of his sons (one being the future King George VI) was interested in taking on *Britannia*, her gear was to be sold off to help out the King George V Fund for Sailors, and the hull was to be scuttled.

Neither expressed an interest. One story told about King Edward VIII, when he was Prince of Wales, had him practising his golf shots off the stern of the old yacht, so uninterested was he in her and her deeds.

So, *Britannia's* gear was sold by auction in Marvin's Yard at Cowes, her mast was presented to the Royal Naval College at Dartmouth, and her spinnaker boom as a flagstaff to Carisbrooke Castle. Her racing flags were given to various yacht clubs round Britain where she had raced.

On 29th June 1936, the hull was launched for a last voyage, out of her berth in the Medina River. Shortly after dawn on 9th July, *HMS Amazon* and *HMS Winchester*, two destroyers, towed her out through the mist around the Isle of Wight to the west, past the Needles, and then, turning south, until they reached St Catherine's light on the very southern tip of the island. There *Britannia* was sunk by explosive charges placed in her bilge. There are two views about this. One is that this was an unparalleled act of vandalism against an object of surpassing beauty; the other is that she had had a modern version of a Viking's funeral, and that her last owner was so tied in mind and deed with her that once he'd gone – and he did offer her to his sons – she had to go too.

With her passing, the world grew a lesser place, of that this writer is certain. Sailors are, as a breed, a superstitious lot. I did not know of the fate of *Britannia* until I came to write this book, but I can say that every time I have passed south of St Catherine's light on much, much lesser ships, I have been struck by the restlessness of the seas there, more than usually turbulent. Could it be that the old yacht is still turning in her grave at the way she was treated after a lifetime of service?

CHAPTER *8*

THE LONG WEEKEND

When the dust cleared over Europe late in 1918 the political landscapes so familiar to the Edwardians had been erased and a strange, unsettled world was in place. Empires had collapsed or been overthrown, some in terrible violence, others merely because they had got in the way of the steamroller of events. There was neither peace nor war, just exhaustion. Amid the wreckage of a once proud and beautiful continent, now scarred by conflict, a new world power from across the Atlantic stood, bemused. If the First World War had changed anything for ever, it was, almost accidentally, the global balance of power. The newly awakened United States found itself where it had never intended to be: at the heart of international affairs. It was an uncomfortable moment for everyone, including the remaining crowned heads of Europe who found a stranger at their hitherto unchallenged table.

Royalty, for the first time since the French Revolution, might have felt more than a chill up their collective spines at the fate of some monarchies: Germany, Russia, Austro-Hungary, the Ottoman Empire – all had been swept away. There were others quickly in place, but the very speed at which they had been installed, along with the antics of the allies at the Versailles Peace Conference, might have given greater cause for concern. Suddenly there were new monarchies in Romania, Yugoslavia (a creation out of hell, if ever there was one), Albania, all countries previously mixed up in the complex Balkan question with the decayed Ottoman Empire.

Bulgaria, an oddity in this chaos, had already gained independence from the Ottomans in 1908; its monarchy staggering on until 1943. The Bulgarian royal family did appear to have use of a vessel on the Black Sea, the *Nadiejda*, as a royal yacht. Built in France, probably at about the turn of the century, she was around 200 feet in length, had a beam of

Detail above President Franklin D Roosevelt fishing on board the *Sequoia*.

Right With the ending of the First World War, the deluge of death across Europe was, for a time, in abeyance. The war had decisively ended the Indian summer of Edwardian decadence in the most terrible way imaginable, and things would never be the same again. The pre-war innocence of halcyon days, racing in the Solent during the Cowes Regatta, would revive in part, but never provide the earlier heady mix of elegance and opulence. Never again would so many members of royal families across Europe mingle. The *Hispania,* racing yacht of King Alphonso of Spain, seen here before the war, epitomises that loss.

23 feet, and a draught of around 12 feet. Her gross tonnage was probably about 700 tons. In neighbouring Romania, under King Carol who'd returned from exile in 1930, the royal family came to acquire a much grander ship, the *Nahlin*. She was built originally for Lady Yule, the Jute millionairess, by John Brown from plans by GL Watson. She was launched in 1930, and was among the last of her kind, for by then diesel was becoming all the rage for yacht engines. At 300 feet long, with a beam of 36 feet, and drawing 15 feet, her two geared steam turbines, oil fired, gave her a top speed of just over 27 knots. Steel hulled, with two masts, she was a magnificent ship.

The story of how she ended up as the Romanian royal yacht is intriguing. It began when she was chartered for an Adriatic cruise in the early 1930s by the Prince of Wales, the future Edward VIII. Among the guests was a Mrs Simpson. This incident was later told to the notorious mistress of King Carol of Romania, Helen Lepescu, who was so taken by it that she persuaded her lover to buy the ship. She was renamed the *Luceafarul*. As a royal yacht she made only one long cruise, to the Aegean, before world events (in the form of the Nazis in Germany, who then exerted a lot of influence in

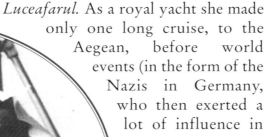

Left The Prince of Wales (later Edward VIII) turns the world on its head on board the *Nahlin*, as he was later to do with the British monarchy.

Inset The Prince of Wales and Mrs Simpson pictured during their Adriatic cruise on the *Nahlin* in the early 1930s.

Left The *Nahlin* in 1930. It was because of her romantic association with the British Prince of Wales and Wallis Simpson that the Romanian King, at the insistence of his mistress, later bought her for his royal yacht, renaming her *Luceafarul*.

Romania, and whose equivalent there, the Iron Guard eventually overran it), helped to ensure the wayward monarch's downfall. Under the post-war communist regime the ship was named *Liberatatea*.

At the opposite end of this scale the Yugoslav royal family opted for a British-built warship. Named the *Dubrovnik*, and built on the Clyde in 1931 by Yarrow, she was 372 feet long, had a beam of 35 feet and drew 12 feet. With a standard displacement of 1,880 tons, and with three Parsons turbines producing 4,200 hp and a top speed of 37 knots, she cut an impressive sight. As a royal yacht she took the King, Alexander I, on official visits to Turkey and Bulgaria in 1933, and to France in 1934. It was there that Alexander I was assassinated by Croat extremists as he drove in state from his ship moored in Marseilles harbour. The Yugoslav monarchy, as with others in the Balkans, did not survive World War II.

South of Yugoslavia, but with its own problems, Greece had set up a republic in 1924 after many years of monarchy. The Greeks had famously gained their own independence from Turkey in 1828, one of their freedom fighters being Lord Byron. The monarchy, however, was restored in 1933 and the elderly King George II came home, probably using the aging steam yacht *Sfakteria* as his royal yacht. Prior to that the Greek monarchs had had use of a British ship, the *Amphitrite*, bought in 1867 and modified to be a royal yacht in 1869. After that came the *Bouboulina* which was renamed the *Amphitrite* after the original was laid up in 1892. This second *Amphitrite* was used as a royal yacht until 1917 when she was finally sunk in an air raid in April 1941 during the German invasion of Greece.

If the Greeks had managed to keep the size and cost of their royal yachts under control, their erstwhile rulers, the Ottomans, had spent the nineteenth century indulging in a series of increasingly splendid vessels. Nothing, however, could match what the republic of Turkey did when it bought the world's largest non-royal yacht and gave it to its saviour and mentor, President Kemal Ataturk, the man credited with single-handedly taking Turkey out of its distant past and hurling it into the twentieth century. The *Savarona* was launched in 1931 by Blohm and Voss from their Bremen yard. She was over 6,000 tons, had a length of 440 feet, a beam of 52 feet and a draught of 20 feet. She was powered by turbines producing 7,200 hp giving her a cruising speed of 17 knots. Her range was over 6,000 miles. In fact this *Savarona* was the third of her name – all built for the American millionairess Emily Cadwallader, whose grandfather had built the Brooklyn Bridge. The first *Savarona* became the *Sequoia*, the US presidential yacht (of which more later). Emily Cadwallader's second *Savarona* (the name comes from a species of Chinese swan) was just under 300 feet long, but the millionairess is reputed to have decided to order a bigger version when she discovered that the yachts of both Julius Forstmann (the *Orion*) and that of JP Morgan (the *Corsair*) were longer.

The third *Savarona*, however, never made it to New York or any of the other US ports where she might have been admired. Mrs

Cadwallader's decision to have it built in Germany when the depression had just bitten deep and hard into the US economy, including into its shipbuilding, meant that questions were raised over her motives – and over her unpaid tax bills. As a result, it was made perfectly clear that, had the *Savarona* ever touched a US port it would have been seized until tax bills were paid, which would have crippled even Mrs Cadwallader.

For her shakedown cruise the last *Savarona* made a tour of Scandinavia, then crossed the Atlantic to Bermuda. Then she went on a series of cruises to the Caribbean, South America and, finally, back to Germany. By this time Mrs Cadwallader was ill, and had put the ship on the market. She turned down an offer from the German Government, who had wanted the ship for Adolf Hitler; instead she agreed to sell it to the Turks, who gave it to their president, Ataturk.

The events which led to this purchase revolve around a visit paid to Turkey by King Edward VIII in 1936. During his visit he sailed with Ataturk on the old Turkish royal yacht *Erthogroul*. So much soot fell from the yacht's funnel that the King's white uniform was ruined. Mortified at their guest's discomfort, the Turks hurriedly scrapped the *Erthogroul* and began an urgent search for a suitable replacement. The *Savarona* was bought for $1 million. She left Southampton for her new life on 24th March 1938.

It was about this time that Ataturk, a very heavy drinker and smoker, was diagnosed as having cirrhosis of the liver – in six months he would be dead. When *Savarona* arrived in Istanbul, in June 1938, he moved on board her at once, staying there until he was close to death. All cabinet meetings were held on board, and Ataturk met King Carol of Romania there when he arrived on a state visit.

The *Savarona* was decommissioned throughout the Second World War, but afterwards she joined the Turkish Navy as a training ship. Ataturk's apartments, though, were kept exactly as they had been during his time on board.

In 1979 a fire caught hold, destroying most of the interior, and her

Top The *Savarona* as she is today. She was the world's biggest royal or state yacht until the *Abdul Aziz* was built in the 1980s.

Above The original maker's nameplate.

Right Views of the lavish interior of the *Savarona* after her refurbishment in the late 1980s. The bedroom shown is that of Kemal Ataturk, and it has been left exactly as it was, a shrine to the man who created modern Turkey.

fate seemed sealed. But she was saved by a Turkish businessman, who later went into partnership with a Japanese consortium to restore the ship to exactly how she was before the war.

In Egypt, between the wars, an additional royal yacht was the *Kassed Kheir*, a paddle-wheeler built by Thorneycroft in Britain for use on the Nile. She was 238 feet long, had a beam of 32 feet, and drew a mere three-and-a-half feet. After King Farouk was deposed she served for a while as an annex to the Semiramis Hotel in Cairo. Fellow Arabian King, Faisal of Iraq, meanwhile, had acquired the *Restless* (renamed *Faisal I*) as a yacht in 1939. She was another GL Watson design, built in 1923 by John Brown. Rigged as a twin-screw schooner, she had a length of 203 feet, a beam of 30 feet and a draught of 13 feet. After the royal family had been overthrown after the war, she was turned into a lighthouse tender. As late as 1968 she was still listed in various international shipping journals.

Mention has been made of the desire by the Germans to find a ship suitable for their leader of the 1930s – Adolf Hitler. Mindful, no doubt, of the glory attaching to his royal predecessors with the *Hohenzollern*, Hitler was possessed of a more militaristic caste of mind. The ship eventually decided upon was the *Grille*, built in 1934 by Blohm and Voss as steel-hulled twin-screw schooner. She was 377 feet in length overall, had a beam of 44 feet and a draught of 11 feet. Her gross tonnage was 3,378 and she could steam at 26 knots. She was named after a much earlier and smaller yacht of the Prussian princes. Translated, *Grille* means caprice.

The *Grille* was of a similar size to the old *Hohenzollern*, but with a much more modern look and diesel engines. She was converted to a minelayer in 1939, surviving the war. She was the dramatic setting for the announcement by Admiral Doenitz on 1st May 1945, of Hitler's suicide. Later she was sailed to the Firth of Forth as part of the British war reparations. She was then sold to a Lebanese businessman, who had wanted to use her for charters. He took her to the USA but found that it would prove too costly. She was scrapped in New Jersey in 1949.

Below The *Kassed Kheir* built for the Egyptian royal family between the wars. With her very shallow draught she was perfect for cruising the Nile.

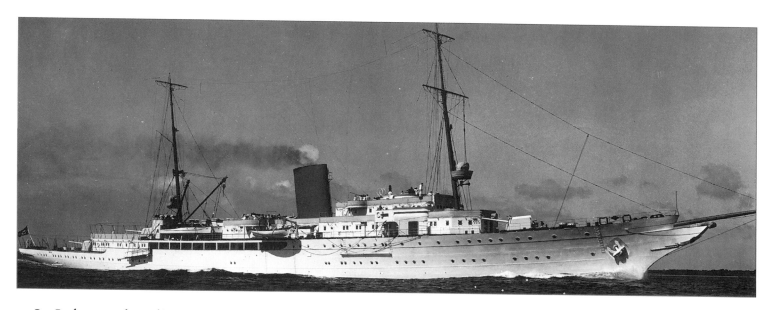

In Italy, another dictator, Mussolini, had come to power on the back of the same turmoil which had eventually allowed Hitler in. But Italy retained a monarchy, although heavily marginalised. In 1925, the *Città di Palermo* was converted to a royal yacht for Victor Emmanuel III, and renamed *Savoia II*. At 390 feet long, with a beam of 49 feet and a draught of 15 feet, she was powered by steam turbines giving her a top speed of 22 knots. Perhaps because of the militaristic regime that the fascists had created, she was classified as a royal warship and carried four naval guns. The King used her a lot, although he also had use of two privately owned yachts as well, both called *Iela* in turn. The *Savoia II* lasted into the Second World War as a gunboat, but she was finally sunk by allied aircraft off Ancona in 1943.

Top The *Grille* used by Adolf Hitler. Converted into a minelayer for the Second World War (as shown here), she was the scene for Admiral Doenitz's announcement, in 1945, that Hitler had committed suicide with his mistress Eva Braun.

Above Hitler inspects his navy.

Despite the apparently inexorable rise of dictatorships across Europe in the 1920s and 1930s, the more stable monarchies and democracies held on, and their rulers kept on doing what they had always done. Britain, in the inter-war period, went through a series of economic crises starting almost as soon as the war ended. As we have seen, King George V gave a boost to the yachting industry by recommissioning *Britannia* after an initial reluctance to be seen indulging in idle pleasures. He remained a King who had strongly held views about extravagance – his Queen, too: for when the King was racing off Cowes, Queen Mary could be found in the antique shops on the island looking for bargains.

It was for reasons of economy that the *Alexandra* was paid off in 1922, that beautiful smaller copy of the third *Victoria and Albert*. She was eventually sold to a Norwegian company where she sailed as a tourist ship around the fjords. Her last voyage as a royal yacht was to take King George and Queen Mary across the Channel on a state visit. *Alexandra* was sunk during the German invasion of Norway in 1940.

Left The aging royal yacht *Victoria and Albert*, originally built in 1899, was used at the Naval Review of 1935.

The third *Victoria and Albert* had been recommissioned in 1919. In 1920 she was used by the King and Queen on a visit to Gourock in the Clyde where the royals inspected the Atlantic Fleet. The yacht then left for Rothesay further down the Clyde where the King met a hundred or so yachtsmen before racing in *Britannia* – and taking first prize. The Queen and Princess Mary were on board, and, although there was a stiff breeze blowing, the Queen didn't on this occasion swear off ever being on the yacht again.

The cruise in the larger royal yacht continued southwards with a visit to the Isle of Man. The royal family disembarked at Holyhead on the Isle of Anglesey, and travelled on through Wales to rejoin the ship at Swansea for the remainder of the voyage back to Portsmouth. This had been in July, and at the end of the month, the yacht was used, just as it had been before the war, for the annual royal visit to Cowes Week, where the King again raced on his beloved *Britannia*. He stayed behind for the Ryde Regatta as well.

The following year the *Victoria and Albert* took the King and Queen to the Channel Islands before being used for a Review of the Fleet in Torbay. The King was ill in 1925, and a longer convalescent cruise was made around the west coast of Italy. It began at Genoa on 20th March and went on until 23rd April. During the cruise the King and Queen spent a week at Leghorn, another in Naples, and visited the Sicilian ports of Messina, Syracuse and Palermo. Then during a later, more serious, illness in 1928–29, the King stayed at Bognor, and naval parties from the royal yacht, anchored offshore, helped with the domestic arrangements in the house.

This pattern of annual short cruises, the visit to Cowes Week, punctuated with Reviews of the Fleet, continued until the King's death in 1936. In July 1932, for instance, the royal yacht was in Weymouth Bay for a Review of the Fleet. She steamed through the lines to a salute

Above King George VI receiving British admirals on the quarter deck of *Victoria and Albert* during the Coronation Review of the Fleet at Spithead on 20th May 1937.

with all the ships manned by cheering sailors. The following day the King inspected officers and men and then went to sea in an aircraft carrier, *HMS Courageous*, to watch flying displays. The royal pulling barge, which had not been used for 20 years, took the King across to *HMS Nelson*, one of the new Washington Treaty size-limited battleships. Every afternoon there were sailing regattas and every evening receptions and dinners on board the royal yacht for flag officers and captains. The Review ended when the royal yacht put to sea with the fleet to watch exercises with destroyers, submarines and aircraft en masse.

It had become a custom, growing since the later years of Queen Victoria's reign, for members of the royal family to go on long overseas visits to parts of the British Empire. The royal yachts were generally ill equipped for these prolonged voyages, so both merchant ships and warships were pressed into service. After the Second World War the new *Britannia*, with her world cruising range, made this unnecessary.

After the First World War, in August 1919, the battlecruiser *Renown* was used by the Prince of Wales (the future Edward VIII) for a visit to Canada. He returned in December, and just three months later he was off again, in the same ship, for a prolonged visit to Australia and New Zealand, returning that October. Meanwhile the Duke of Connaught used the battleship *Malaya* to go to India in December 1920 to open the Provincial Legislative Council there.

In 1921 the Prince of Wales visited India, again in *Renown*, and in 1927 she was used by the Duke and Duchess of York (soon to be King George VI and Queen Elizabeth) for a six-month cruise to Australia to open the parliament at Canberra, and to New Zealand. The Duchess left behind an infant daughter of six months, the future Queen Elizabeth II.

Below HMS Renown, used by the Duke and Duchess of York (*inset*), later George VI and Queen Elizabeth, for a visit to Australia and New Zealand in 1927.

The British use of warships as temporary official ships, a kind of extension of the royal yacht idea, was mirrored, as we have seen, by a number of other monarchies, for one reason or another. It was also employed from time to time by the United States.

Theodore Roosevelt, before the First World War, had cruised in the *USS Louisiana* to Panama to view the then wonder of the modern age, the new canal. The enlisted men had given Mrs Roosevelt a silver Tiffany vase on their return. In the 1930s Franklin D Roosevelt took a trip of 14,000 miles on the *USS Houston* to Haiti, Colombia, Panama and Hawaii. In 1936 he voyaged to Argentina in the *USS Indianapolis* to attend the Pan-American Peace Conference there. On the way they heard about the abdication crisis in Britain and, over dinner, several of the President's party, including FDR, made bets on the outcome. When they finally heard what had happened, FDR insisted his betting slip be destroyed. 'If it gets out what I thought, there'd be war,' he has been quoted as saying.

His use of the *USS Indianapolis* would hardly be worth mentioning except for one of those twists of history which give fate a lever on reason. In 1945 it was the *USS Indianapolis* which took one of the two atomic bombs out to the forward Pacific airbase of Trinian from which it would be flown. The mission was so secret that no other ships or aircraft were told of the cruiser's whereabouts. On the way back, on 29th July, with the same orders in place, the ship was torpedoed. A large number survived the attack, but rescue was slow in coming because of the secrecy of the voyage. Over the next few days, most of the survivors

Top West meets East: President Roosevelt in conversation with the King of Saudi Arabia on board the *USS Quincy*, in the Great Bitter Lake, Egypt, February 1945.

Above FDR relaxing aboard the *Sequoia* in the company of Marguerite Le Hand and Captain Wilson Brown, his naval aide.

Top The Sequoia, much-loved yacht for eight US presidents from Hoover to Ford.

were attacked and killed by a huge pack of sharks that had gathered around their liferafts. The *Indianapolis* was the last major allied warship sunk in the Second World War.

The aging but beautiful *Mayflower* had been withdrawn as a presidential yacht in 1931, and not replaced until 1933 by the *Sequoia* (originally built for the Cadwalladers in 1925).

Both before and after the commissioning of the *Sequoia*, FDR also enjoyed using the much larger yacht of Vincent Astor. The *Nourmahal*, at 263 feet long, was somewhat larger than the *Sequoia* at 99 feet on the waterline. During a very short cruise on board *Nourmahal* in 1935, the President is reported as questioning Astor as to the cost of putting the ship into commission for so short a trip. Astor replied that his ship was always in commission, to which FDR replied: 'then I guess we'll have to increase the taxes on the rich'.

The President had watched the America's Cup challenge from the deck of the *Nourmahal* in 1934, as she was then the flagship of the New York Yacht Club. In 1935 he went on a 13-day cruise to the Bahamas, the occasion for his remarks to Vincent Astor. The log of that voyage makes interesting reading, given the way in which today's presidents, with their awesome responsibilities, have to stay constantly in touch with events back in Washington. The entries are from the actual log kept for FDR by his naval aide, Captain Wilson Brown. They embarked from Jacksonville, Florida:

'Wednesday March 27: During the night messages were received indicating that the Duke and Duchess of Kent were at Cat Cay on board

Left Astor's yacht *Nourmahal,* from which President Roosevelt had just landed in Miami when an attempted assassination took place in February 1933.

the American yacht, MOANA, that the Governor and his wife would arrive at noon and that Vincent Astor would have a luncheon on board the NOURMAHAL. Both destroyers manned the rail on approaching the anchorage. The FARRAGUT went alongside NOURMAHAL and the President transferred to NOURMAHAL at 1020 with two Secret Service. Captains Brown and McIntire and three Secret Service remained aboard FARRAGUT.

'After the official luncheon the NOURMAHAL and FARRAGUT got underway (at 1430) for Lobos Cay where arrangements were made with the Pan American Airways to stop on their regular trip to Miami to transfer Mr James Roosevelt – speed 14 knots – distance – 240 miles.

'CLAXTON proceeded to Miami to act as radio relay and plane guard. A severe strain on communication was experienced owing to long coded despatches from CLAXTON – decoders worked almost all night.'

This problem with communications continued, with the direct radio phone lines also proving a problem, as well as getting the mail out and back using seaplanes. One of these, carrying urgent messages back had to make a forced landing 12 miles out from Miami. She then had to be found by the coastguard and towed in.

Back on the *Nourmahal,* the President was finding the fishing 'disappointing'. By 5th April, however, Captain Brown reported that they had found 'many interesting small fish to be kept for an aquarium'. His summary of the trip is given here:

'The cruise was a complete success in that the President had two weeks of rest, recreation and outdoor exercise. The mild climate of the Bahamas was a pleasant break from the raw weather of Washington. The President, while still directing the affairs of State, and being kept constantly informed by radio and mail of the affairs of Government and the international situation, had a complete break from the normal

Inset above President Roosevelt at the helm of the schooner *Amberjack II* during a cruise off Cape Cod in June 1933.

Right inset The schooner *Sewanee,* skippered by President Roosevelt and manned by his sons, James, John and Franklin Jr, leaving Pulpit Harbour, Maine for a vacation cruise in July 1936.

Right Relaxing with guests aboard the *Potomac* on a cruise on the Hudson River.

139

THE LONG WEEKEND

office procedure. He spent many hours each day in an open boat under the most restful conditions; i.e., the President's final press dispatch:

'"We hugged azure skies, golden sands, turquoise depths, lush pampas, intriguing inlets, basking lizards, swooping seagulls, winking stars, snapping turtles, lovely doves, verdant seaweeds, and perfect serenity."'

The *Nourmahal* came to a sad end in November 1964 when, then owned by a Texan oilman who had planned to convert her into a floating hotel, she caught fire, capsized and sank in Texas City harbour.

Roosevelt made two cruises in the *Sequoia*, one in 1933 and the other in 1935, around the Potomac river and Chesapeake Bay areas. He used the *Sequoia* from time to time to receive visitors, or to take them for short trips on the river, as in April 1933 when the British Prime Minister Ramsay MacDonald was on board. *Sequoia*, designed for the very rich Cadwalladers, was said to be breathtakingly beautiful. Over a keel and frame of oak, her hull was planked in Honduras mahogany. The decks and deckhouse were of Burmese teak while interior panelling was also of Honduras mahogany. All the deck hardware was of chrome-plated bronze. Of 110 tons, her cruising speed at nine knots gave her a range of 1,400 miles. In all, she was to be used by eight presidents, starting with Herbert Hoover who, as a keen fisherman, had taken her down to Key Largo. Intriguingly, it is

said that when Eleanor wasn't with FDR on the various short trips he took aboard *Sequoia*, a mistress was. If so, it confirms that state yachts have the same appeal as royal yachts have, in various locations, for the more personal kind of 'affairs of state'. FDR is also supposed to have relished losing his secret-service escorts in the fogs which plague Chesapeake Bay. To accommodate the wheelchair Roosevelt used, a doorless elevator was built into the aft bulkhead of the 38-foot saloon. Also for his comfort the upper deck was fitted with removable glass panels in 1938.

The *Potomac*, still sailing on the waters of San Fransisco Bay in 1997, was built in 1934 as the coastguard cutter *Electra*, chasing gun-runners along the east coast in her short career as a warship. She was converted to an official yacht partly because the White House staff thought the *Sequoia* was too hazardous for a wheelchair-using President, especially because of all that wood and the risk of fire. The *Potomac* is 165 feet long, has a beam of just under 24 feet and a draught of eight feet. She is of 450 tons, but was never considered particularly good for open waters. After the Second World War began, this ban was insisted upon by the US Navy. She was a comfortable ship, for all her limitations at sea. Aft on the main deck there is a large covered lounge, equipped, when she was a presidential yacht, with heavy cushions and easy chairs; in US Navy-speak this was the fantail, and it was used for serving meals, for reading and relaxation, and for fishing. Just forward of this in the deck house, which was added when the *Electra* was converted, was the main dining saloon and the presidential staterooms.

Above and right The *Potomac* carrying President Roosevelt, King George VI and Queen Elizabeth to Mount Vernon during a state visit in 1939. The Royal Standard is flying from her mainmast.

In 1939 the *Potomac* made a historic short voyage with King George VI and Queen Elizabeth on board, during the first visit of a reigning British monarch to the United States. At her mainmast she flew the Royal Standard. In August 1941, on a more serious journey, she ostensibly set off on a fishing trip with the President on board. In fact she made a rendezvous with a cruiser which took him to the coast off Newfoundland where he met Winston Churchill. The two men hammered out what became known as the Atlantic Charter, affirming the rights of peoples to self-government and freedom. To complete the ruse, while this historic meeting was taking place, the *Potomac* cruised off Maine, a crew member posing on deck dressed in the President's familiar cape and fedora.

During the Second World War, royal yachts were either laid up or pressed urgently into service as naval vessels – only some would survive, like their owners. The greatest changes wrought by the Second World War were, again, in Europe, with the destruction of Germany and the rise of the Soviet Union's influence across Eastern Europe and the entire world. In the shadow of communist orthodoxy lay the ever-present threat of nuclear weapons. Their power and range meant that, perforce, the world was about to become a global village.

In all these huge alterations to the way the world organised its affairs, royalty, as well as its trappings, would have to make its own, often painful, adjustments. The pace of change itself was changing. It meant that for the first time royal families and heads of government would find it easier, and more congenial, to travel by air.

CHAPTER 9

FROM EMPIRES TO GLOBAL VILLAGE

The 50-plus years since the end of the Second World War have witnessed a huge number of changes in the world; some might have been foreseen in 1945, others could not have been imagined. It is difficult to know what historians will pick out as the most important changes, but taking a guess, the extent to which huge numbers of people now travel all over the world might be among them. This increased mobility has been solidly based on the triple foundations of developments in air transport, increased disposable income and more leisure time. Significantly, people at large see this as a right, not a privilege. Although there is still a fair amount of old-fashioned privilege to be seen, one of its adjuncts, deference, has collapsed. At the pinnacle of a system of privilege and deference, previously thought unassailable, royal families in the developed world have had to cut their cloth to suit the fashion. Some have been more successful at this than others but, by and large, royalty has – to use a modern idiom – downsized, both in its extent and its ambitions.

Some of this was coming before the war. In Britain, hit hard by the long, wearisome years of the Great Depression of the 1930s, discussion over a replacement for the aging *Victoria and Albert* had been under way since at least 1937. An early drawing, sent to Buckingham Palace for King George VI to mull over, is of the royal yacht *Britannia*, eventually to be built 16 years later. Because of the sensitivity over the economic situation, it had been decided, at that early stage, to make her convertible, in theory at least, into a hospital ship in times of war. In the event, the first ship used by the royals after the war was *HMS Vanguard*, a warship, when they travelled to South Africa.

Detail above Princess Elizabeth on *HMS Vanguard* for the royal tour of South Africa in 1947.

Right Two of the huge ships belonging to the royal families of the Gulf states. The Saudi Arabian-owned *Abdul Aziz (above); Lady Moura, (below)* believed to be owned by the wife of one of the Saudi royals.

In 1947 the royal family made a state visit to South Africa.

Above left HMS *Vanguard* arriving in Portsmouth at the end of the tour.
Above right Princess Margaret runs for cover.
Inset Princess Elizabeth enjoys life on board on her 21st birthday.
Below right Arriving back home.
Below The Queen's day cabin.
Below left The King and Queen, watched by their daughters, have a shooting match.
Left Informality was the watchword.

When the war ended, the economic state of Britain was close to catastrophic. The effect of fighting two global wars within 30 years had wiped out sterling balances abroad, annihilated a large part of Britain's position as the world's leading trading nation, and caused immense hardship to the British people. Few would have dared to state the obvious at that time: Britain, once a global power, would have to come to terms with being at best a medium power in the future and would, within a generation, have to join with the rest of Europe in trying to create a collective future, or continue to decline.

The grand illusion, to which all politicians subscribed, was that nothing had changed. It would take decades before the penny dropped; meanwhile the old show would run and run. Circumstances were changing, though, and dramatically. The jewel in the crown of the British Empire, India, was about to become independent, and many other nations would follow that lead in the 1950s and 1960s. Some would just break away in the post-war period, like South Africa, beginning to put into place its own twisted scheme of apartheid. And it was to South Africa that the royal family first went on a state visit after the war in 1947, not long before Princess Elizabeth married.

It was because the old *Victoria and Albert* could never have stood up to such a long voyage, and because no other merchant ship could be spared in the desperately austere days of post-war Britain, that the royal family embarked on the pride of the British fleet, the newly commissioned – and last – battleship *HMS Vanguard*. With a displacement tonnage of 51,420, and over 800 feet, packing eight 15-inch guns as her main armament, she was a magnificently obsolete example of her kind.

Her short history sums up this changing world. First ordered in 1941 it proved beyond the capacity of overstretched British shipyards to finish her until the war had ended. Totally superseded by air power and submarine technology, let alone the still-hardly-understood effects of nuclear weapons, she never fired her guns in anger. She was sold for scrap in 1960 after spending years 'mothballed' in a remote Scottish loch.

Taking the royal family to South Africa was probably the *Vanguard*'s finest hour. It was the first peacetime voyage made by royalty in a warship since 1927 when the then Duke and Duchess of York (now the King and Queen) went in *HMS Renown* to Australia. It was also the first time either of the royal Princesses had been abroad, and the photographs of them playing deck games with dozens of young naval officers suggest that they felt able to relax.

The *Vanguard*, which had been blessed by Princess Elizabeth in 1946, had had a number of urgent changes made to its internal and external arrangements to provide a semblance of luxury. The shelter deck was converted to royal accommodation. Normally this was the admiral's quarters. It was made entirely self-contained with its own galley and switchboard. Some furnishings were brought from the last *Victoria and Albert*. One external change was to weld a floor and a windshield on top of B turret to provide a very crude, if well-intentioned, veranda for

Right The *Gothic*, the last merchant ship used by the British royal family for a state visit, ready for its Coronation world tour in 1954.

Below The interior of the *Medina*, a P&O steamer, adapted for a royal visit to India in 1911 by King George V and Queen Mary: the royal smoking room *(below)* and the Queen's bedroom *(right)*.

secluded sunbathing. The escorting ships included two cruisers, an aircraft carrier and a destroyer. It took 17 days each way to reach South Africa.

The lack of a royal yacht, by then ordered but shelved until the economic situation improved, was felt again just after Elizabeth became Queen. For her Coronation Review of the Fleet in 1953 she had to use an elderly and hastily converted frigate, *HMS Surprise.* In another odd twist, this elderly ship had once been the *Margarita* and then the *Alberta,* King Leopold of the Belgians' yacht. The new Queen, unwittingly perhaps (or did the Admiralty know its history books?), welcomed her fleet aboard the remains of a classic Victorian steam yacht.

That same year, when the new Queen and the Duke of Edinburgh set sail on their world tour of the Commonwealth (the hoped-for successor to the Empire), they had to make use of a merchant ship chartered from Shaw Saville. The *Gothic* cost £40,000 a month, and the bill for painting her hull white was sent to the Palace. This was very different from the time, in 1911, when the P&O liner the *Medina* had been lent to the royal family for its maiden voyage when it took King George V and Queen Mary to the Delhi Durbar.

Like the use of warships from time to time, merchant ship charters had been used where a royal yacht, for one reason or another, had been unable to

Above The *Balmoral Castle* was used by the Duke and Duchess of Connaught for a trip to South Africa for the opening of the first parliament in 1910, part of a tradition of using merchant ships for royal visits to parts of the British Empire.

fulfil the task at hand. The Prince of Wales had used *Serapis* in 1875–76 for an earlier trip to India. The next Prince of Wales and his wife had used the *Ophir* for another trip to India in 1901, a voyage that continued right around the world ending in Newfoundland. Nine years later the *Balmoral Castle*, a Union Castle liner, took Queen Victoria's third son and his wife, the Duke and Duchess of Connaught, to open the first South African Union parliament. The *Gothic* has the distinction of being the last ship used by a reigning monarch over an extended period as a royal ship (rather than yacht) because *Britannia* had already been launched by Queen Elizabeth in the April before her Coronation.

The clash of merchant marine with both the ways of the British Admiralty and those of the royal family, led to a few spats. One, related by *Gothic*'s master, David Aitchison, was when he was asked to take the Sunday divine service. 'All went well, until the end,' he recalled. 'Instead of singing one verse of the national anthem as was always my custom, we were to sing, kneeling, the last verse of "Eternal Father strong to save". I thought I had better announce this, so when giving the number for the last hymn I said "After the blessing we will sing the last verse of the hymn, kneeling".' But when Aitchison came to read the blessing, to his surprise everyone knelt for this. He wondered whether he ought to be standing while the Queen was kneeling, but it was too late. At that point the Royal Marine band went straight into the voluntary, entirely missing out the last verse. No-one moved. He then saw the Queen dig her husband in the ribs, and both got up to leave, easing everyone's embarrassment. The bandmaster, over a drink later, was admitting nothing.

Gothic met *Britannia* in Malta on her return, her master noting: 'She rather disappointed me. I had been expecting something very exceptional, a ship of such beauty that she would sit the water with the grace of a seabird. The *Britannia* fell short of that. Her lines and design were, I thought, conventional and unimaginative, while the general appearance had been spoiled by the box-like deckhouses on her upper deck.'

On the other side of the Atlantic, by this time, President Eisenhower had inherited the largest US presidential yacht ever, the *Williamsburg,* used by President Truman, but he decided to decommission her, relying instead on two much smaller motor yachts which had acted as tenders to the *Williamsburg.* The *Sequoia* was hardly used at all. The smaller boats were the *Leonore* and the *Margie,* which he renamed respectively *Barbara Ann* and *Susie-E*, after his two granddaughters. The former motor yacht had been built by the Defoe Boat and Motor Works of Bay City Michigan. In length 92 feet, with a beam of 16-and-a-half feet, she had a long shelter deck, very much in a 1930s style. It is clear from pictures of her that she was never intended for use at sea. The *Susie-E* was 64 feet long with a beam of 14-and-a-half feet. Built at the Fisher Boat Works in Detroit, she was made available for members of Ike's cabinet; the *Barbara Ann* was used by him and his family for vacations in 1957 and 1960 at Newport.

To return to 1945 and the *Williamsburg* for a moment, she had been the replacement for the *Potomac.* Built in 1930 by the Bath Iron Works, Maine, she displaced 1,920 tons, had a length overall of 244 feet and a beam of 36 feet, drawing 16 feet. Her twin diesel engines could provide 16 knots flat out. She was nothing like as elegant as her predecessors but she suited the sombre mood of the late 1940s when the United States had come to terms with its new and lasting global role, and the growing threat posed by the Soviet Union and her allies. She lent a subdued but war-like aura to the presidency, matched neither before nor since.

Much later, but still in the middle of the Cold War, the election of John F Kennedy to the White House in 1960 brought with it the promise of a new dawn. It brought a new style to the President's office and a breath of fresh air to the household. Jack Kennedy took over three yachts, renaming the two smaller ones the *Honey Fitz* (after his maternal grandfather, a former mayor of Boston) and the *Patrick J* (after

Below left The large US presidential yacht *Williamsburg* anchored in Hampton Roads, in use after the Second World War.

Below right President Truman sunbathing on the *Williamsburg* as she passes through the Chesapeake and Delaware Canal.

Left Jack the lad: Kennedy enjoyed sailing yachts, like FDR before him.

Inset right Kennedy managed to put most of the cares of office behind him when he was at sea.

Right With his two children, Caroline and John Jnr, aboard *Honey Fitz*.

Below British Prime Minister Harold Macmillan and President Kennedy board the *Honey Fitz* for strategy talks and a cruise down the Potomac River.

his paternal grandfather). With his wife and small children he made a number of cruises on *Honey Fitz* on the Potomac, to Hyannis Port and in Narransett Bay. In 1961 he met the British Prime Minister Harold Macmillan on board.

The Kennedys also used the *Sequoia*. On Jack's 46th birthday they held a candlelit dinner aboard. Among the 30 guests, one, very drunk, damaged a painting given to him by Jackie. Kennedy also used this yacht for a number of cabinet meetings and conferences, as well as for other 'entertainment', some of which, no doubt, involved the many women he had affairs with. Drink and, if recent accounts are to be believed, drugs supplied from seizures by the FBI, would have been much in evidence. Quite possibly with no trace of irony in her action, Jackie had had an extra hard bed installed in *Sequoia* to ease Jack's constant back pains, the result of his war injuries after his patrol boat PT109 sank in the Pacific. The *Honey Fitz* had also made 'bachelor' cruises with the President and his cronies on board, to Palm Beach.

The death of John F Kennedy and the traumas of the 1960s did not prevent Lyndon Johnson from undertaking what amounted to a major refit on the *Sequoia*. New walnut panelling for the presidential

stateroom, two other staterooms redone in bleached ash, and a conversion of FDR's lift into a bar, were among the changes. Johnson also had the shower altered, complaining that he bumped his head every time he used it (he was six foot three inches tall). It was on *Sequoia* that members of the British royal family were entertained, not in his Texan bar-room style quarters, but around the Honduras mahogany dining table with its built-in sherry decanters and its $5,000 Irish linen tablecloth. The *Sequoia*'s engines were also replaced at this time by twin GM diesels, each of 260 hp, and the latest electronic navigation aids were added to the bridge.

Nixon used the *Sequoia* more than 80 times in his presidency, cruising on the Potomac. He entertained Leonid Brezhnev and other Soviet leaders on board during one of the rounds of the SALT talks. *Sequoia* was also lent to Emperor Hirohito when he visited Washington. At a dinner Nixon sat Prince Charles strategically next to his unmarried daughter, Tricia, while on deck the crew were unwittingly flying the Union flag upside down.

Nixon carried on the tradition of renaming the smaller yachts, both for his daughters. The *Honey Fitz* became the *Patricia,* and the *Patrick J* the *Julie,* but both were shortly afterwards sold off as an economy measure. It was on the *Sequoia,* the sole remaining presidential yacht, that Nixon announced to his stunned family that he was resigning.

Gerald Ford entertained *Apollo* astronauts on this same stately yacht, but Jimmy Carter never even went aboard before he ordered her sold at public auction in 1977, claiming she was costing the US taxpayer $800,000 a year to maintain. Although Ronald Reagan had lived by the ocean in California before moving to the White House, he didn't seek a state yacht for his use. Neither did Bush, although a keen yachtsman. And neither has Bill Clinton. Twenty years have passed since the last US presidential yacht, and it may be fair to say that, after 130 years, the United States has ended its love affair with this kind of transport.

In Europe that love affair has in general continued, but in often muted tones outside Britain. One country that joined this royal yacht club, belatedly, was Norway, when the nation bought its King, Haakon, Tommy Sopwith's yacht *Philante* when the King returned after the war. Sopwith, the millionaire aircraft manufacturer, had had *Philante* built by Camper and Nicolson in Southampton in 1937 as the support ship in his efforts to win the America's Cup with his yacht *Endeavour*. *Philante* was named for his wife Phyllis and himself (Phil-and-T with an 'e' added to the end). At 260 feet, with a beam of around 37 feet, drawing 15 feet, she has a cruising speed of 15 knots, and a top speed of 17 knots.

In her short career before the war she had visited Norway, and made a round-the-world voyage. During the war *Philante* was an escort vessel serving in the Atlantic and on the west coast of Africa. She had been handed back to Sir Tommy Sopwith in 1946. A public subscription across Norway raised the entire sum of £250,000 with which to buy her for the King for his 75th birthday. She was renamed *Norge*, by King Haakon, on 7th June 1948. She has been used by the kings of Norway and their families ever since. In 1997 she was, as she has been frequently, riding to her anchor off Cowes for the King to race in the regatta.

Norge was badly damaged by fire in 1985, and in her rebuild she was modernised to meet current standards for a worldwide ocean-going yacht (she has a range of 6,000 miles). She is crewed by eight officers, 12 petty officers and 45 ratings of the Norwegian Navy. Her extensive use by the Norwegian royals in the summer has meant her being thought of by that far northern nation of seafarers as their King's floating palace.

Right The Danish royal yacht since the 1930s, *Dannebrog* in Greenland for an official visit in 1989.

Below The *Norge*, formerly the *Philante*, Tommy Sopwith's yacht. An aging but still beautiful diesel yacht, she has been the Norwegian royal yacht since 1947, when she was bought as a present by the grateful people of Norway, for their King.

The Danish royal family still has use of another survivor from the 1930s, the *Dannebrog*, the second ship of that name. Built by the Royal Dockyard, Copenhagen, for King Christian X, she is 207 feet in length, has a beam of 34 feet and draws 12 feet. The *Dannebrog* is powered by twin diesels, and has a Thames Measurement tonnage of 1,070. She looks very much like the classic Victorian steam yacht, except that she has a broken sheer line. The *Dannebrog*, like the *Norge*, is probably the last of her kind.

The other Scandinavian monarchy, Sweden, now has no official royal yacht, just a privately owned motor yacht. In Holland, too, the Dutch royal family has relinquished its aging royal yacht, using naval ships instead when on official business. *Piet Hein,* the last royal yacht, had been given to the then Princess Juliana and Prince Bernhard as a wedding gift from the people of Holland in 1937. Just over 100 feet in length, with a beam of 19 feet and drawing five feet, she had a Thames Measurement tonnage of 151. Never really a sea-going vessel, she was mainly used on the extensive waterways of the Netherlands for pleasure cruises as well as for civic functions. Queen Beatrice also owned a traditional Dutch sailing yacht, *De Groene Draeck*, given to her as an 18th birthday present. She used to delight in sailing it, and it has a direct lineage to the *jachts* so loved by King Charles II. In design, based on the Friesland Island fishing boats, *De Groene Draeck* was 49 feet long, had a beam of 15 feet and drew three-and-a-half feet (she used traditional leeboards for extra 'bite' in the water).

Inset above The Swedes no longer have an official royal yacht, but King Carl Gustav and Queen Silvia made use of a state barge on the occasion of their marriage.

Further south in Europe there was, post-war, a continuation of a long line of royal yachts in Monaco. Prince Rainier and Princess Grace enjoyed the use of the 133-foot, 80-ton *Deo Juvante* (and its successor *Deo Juvante II*); their children that of *Stalca*, whose name derived from the first two initials of their names. Princess Caroline bought *Pacha III* in 1990 for her private use.

In Spain, once the long dictatorship of Franco had ended, with the monarchy restored, the Spanish royals made much use in the summer of the old dictator's yacht, the *Azor*, entertaining friends and relatives in the western Mediterranean around Majorca. In Greece, which became a republic in the 1970s, the state had no official yacht until Aristotle Onassis, the enigmatic ship owner, willed his yacht *Christina* to the state in 1978; she is now named the *Argo*. She has had little use since then, and has been put up for auction several times without success.

Top Prince Rainier and Princess Grace coming ashore from the *Deo Juvante II* in Monaco. The Monagasgue royals have enjoyed a wide range of yachts down the years.

Above left The *Pacha III* owned by Princess Caroline.

Above right Prince Rainier aboard a sailing yacht in the South of France.

Right Spanish dictator Franco fishing on board *Azor*, his state yacht from 1949. When the monarchy was restored she became the Spanish royal yacht.

Right King Juan Carlos at the helm of *Fortuna* with ex-King Constantine of Greece.

Below The Spanish royal family entertain the Prince and the Princess of Wales and their children.

The period between 1945 and 1990 was the time of the communist regimes in Eastern Europe. Most were dour, faceless governments with few memorable moments. The exception, because its future had been left open by the Yalta Conference between Roosevelt and Stalin, was Yugoslavia. Now much in the news since the collapse of communism, it was held together from 1945 by the will of one man – Tito – its wartime partisan leader. Tito could never have been described as faceless, and his larger-than-life character was reflected by his love of beautiful things – including women and yachts.

Tito managed to own a number of yachts down the years, entertaining his frequent foreign guests on them. The *Jabranka* was built in Trieste just before the war. At 213 feet long and powered by twin diesels, she could make 18 knots. The *Krajina* was a riverboat, used for cruises on the Danube. She had a tonnage of 250, a length of 164 feet and drew only four feet. But there were also the *Galeb, Podgorka, Kozara* and *Istranka*. In 1992 the Croatian Government put the *Podgorka* on the market at $1.3 million. She had, in her time as a state yacht, entertained Queen Elizabeth II, King Hussein of Jordan, Queen Margarethe of Denmark, Haile Selassie of Ethiopia and Colonel Gaddafi of Libya among many others. Able to reach 32 knots, she was one of the fastest and most luxurious of these ships. *Istranka* is currently at the Valdettaro yard in La Spezia partly restored. As a footnote to this story, also at anchor in the bay is the ex-*USS Williamsburg*, now in poor condition.

Gaddafi, that long survivor of Libya's turbulent politics, had his own yacht, the *Hannibal*, on which to relax, although very little is known about how this yacht has been used, secrecy being the watchword of much of Middle Eastern and Arab politics.

Top The *Podgorka*, one of several yachts used by President Tito of former Yugoslavia.

Above Tito with friends and fish.

Left The *Istranka*, another of Tito's yachts.

Outside of Europe and the United States, a scattering of royal or state yachts were to be found. In the Philippines, immediately after the war, the President used a former US Navy fleet minesweeper, the *Quest*, renamed the *Apo*. She was of 850 displacement tons, 184 feet long with a beam of 33 feet and a draught of 10 feet. In 1958 she was replaced by *Lapu-Lapu*, a war reparations ship built in Japan, and named somewhat luridly after the local chief who had killed Magellan in 1521. She was then renamed *Roxas* after the first president of the Philippines, then *The President* after Marcos, and since 1975 the *Ang Pangulo*. Since the demise of President Marcos and his shoe-obsessed wife, Imelda, she has been converted into an attack transport. She has a standard tonnage of 2,239, is 258 feet long with a beam of 43 feet and a draught of 21 feet.

The Siamese royal family had kept a number of exquisitely decorated state barges on the rivers as well as their larger sea-going ships. Today, as the Thai royal family, they have use of a survey ship, the *Chanthara*, of 870 displacement tons, and 230 feet long. She was built in 1960.

To the north, the Japanese have retained an inscrutable image. It is hard to establish whether the imperial family used royal yachts in any way, and whether the royal family today has use of a special vessel. Two possibles are the *Hiyodori*, listed as an 'auxiliary special service yacht' and the smaller *Matsunami* 'used for VIPs' in the official Navy List. The *Hiyodori* is of 445 displacement tons, 197 feet long with a beam of 23 feet and a draught of eight feet. With a speed of 20 knots, she has a range of 3,000 miles.

If the Japanese remain inscrutable, some of the other royal families who retain yachts are

Inset King Bhumibol of Thailand aboard a state barge.

Below left Thai state barge.

Below right King Bhumibol in a less formal setting with his sailing boat.

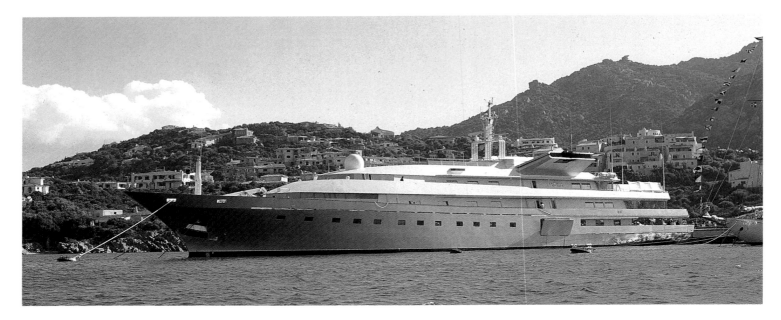

actively hostile to any information leaking out about their vessels. There is an air of farce about this as some are among the biggest, not to say the flashiest, yachts afloat – as they are designed to be. The Sultan of Brunei, whose court and family's alleged antics in his feudally run state were the subject of considerable interest in 1997, had use of the *Khalifah*. His younger brother had the 180-foot *Tits*, with its two tenders *Nipple 1* and *Nipple 2*. Some idea of the attitude of this royal family to life on top of the wealth tree was given in 1996 when the Sultan ordered a new yacht, to be built in Europe. One of its principal specifications was that it had to be larger than the largest yacht owned by the King of Saudi Arabia.

The Saudi royal family had been able to indulge themselves, along with rulers all around the Persian Gulf, ever since they discovered the 'oil weapon' in 1973 and hiked the price to a level that provided them with untold riches. All around them, ever since the 1950s, royal families had toppled – in Egypt, Iraq and Iran. They clung on, locked into a way of life they had known for centuries, but now able to indulge in Western living out of sight of their subjects. In all this, the often huge royal yachts they had built were an integral part. The largest of the Saudi yachts, *Abdul Aziz*, remains the biggest in the world, bigger than *Britannia* by 70 feet. She is 482 feet long, has a beam of 60 feet and a draught of 16 feet. She was built in Copenhagen in 1984. *Al Salamah*, another of the Saudi royal yachts, was built in 1973 as the *Atlantis* by Hellenic Shipyards for Stavros Niarchos. She was sold in 1978 to the Saudis and managed for them by John Latsis, who manages many of the Middle Eastern royal yachts. She was first renamed *Prince Abdul Aziz* and then *Al Salamah*. A number of Middle Eastern yachts, such as the *Lady Moura*, are not listed as royal yachts at all, to retain privacy.

Al Menwar is used as the Qatar state yacht, normally based in Palma, Majorca. She is in commission throughout the summer season in the Mediterranean.

Above The *Nabila*, now renamed *Kingdom*, one of the Saudi royal yachts. She had previously been owned by the arms dealer Khashoggi.

Above right The *Abdul Aziz* in 1997, soon to be ousted as the world's largest royal yacht.

Centre right *Al Salamah*, another of the Saudi royal yachts.

Below right *Al Menwar*, one of the royal yachts of the Gulf state of Qatar.

Egypt had become a republic in 1952, when the last king, Farouk, sailed away into exile on the aging, but still beautiful *Mahroussa*. In Iraq, things were bloodier, a tradition which Saddam Hussein has, more recently, kept up. He, however, has managed to own at least two yachts, the *Qadissiya Saddam* and the *Zinat al Bihaar*. The Shah of Iran, before he was deposed, had the *Chahsavar* as a yacht. Built in the Netherlands in 1936, she was 176 feet long, had a beam of 26 feet and a draught of 10 feet. She was kept for the Shah's use on the waters of the Caspian Sea where Iran borders Russia.

By the 1990s there was a general trend among the world's remaining royal families, excluding the Gulf states, for a more modest profile, reflected in their choice and use of any royal yachts they might still have. Many, as we have seen, had given up the idea altogether. Republics, too, as conscious as everyone of the calling to account for extravagances, real or perceived, had also forgone any pleasure implied in the ownership and use of anything so hedonistic as a yacht.

Outside their use of *Britannia*, the current British royal family had in part gone back to the simple pleasures of small yacht or even dinghy racing. This was first taken up by Prince Philip in the Solent, racing *Coweslip*, a wedding gift from the people of Cowes, or the 29-foot Dragon-class racer, *Bluebottle*, and later the yacht *Bloodhound*. This interest has helped to encourage the sport. Prince Charles seems less enthusiastic than his father, although he appears to have toyed for a time with windsurfing.

With a return to small yacht racing in Britain, the wheel has finally come full circle. The sight of Prince Philip, or his daughter, the Princess Royal, who also has raced yachts, beating hard against the wind, spray flying, the yacht heeled with her lee rail under water, would be one King Charles II would have recognised and applauded. Over the large-scale *Britannia*, he might have been less enthusiastic. It is to the life and death of this most-familiar of royal yachts that we finally turn. In her long career *Britannia* has always been a ship apart.

Above The *Mahroussa*, with the exiled King Farouk of Egypt on board, after he had fled the revolution which brought Nasser to power in 1952.

Below and opposite Since the 1950s members of the British royal family, notably Prince Philip (*opposite*), have tried dinghy and small yacht sailing. Princess Anne (now the Princess Royal) and Prince Charles have also tried their hands; Prince Charles, for a time, had a go at windsurfing (*below*).

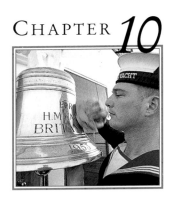

CHAPTER 10

A SHIP APART

Unlike any of her predecessors, *Britannia* has had the world as her stage. From the beginning her voyages have included exotic faraway places. The new Queen Elizabeth and her consort used her as an ocean-going ship to visit, in the first few years of her reign, many of her overseas colonies and dominions. By 1960, six years into her sealife, *Britannia* had already been on a world tour with the Duke of Edinburgh, as well as to Canada, most of Scandinavia, the Caribbean, West Africa, and islands in the Pacific. As time went by, most of the inhabited world could have seen her, at one time or another, sailing by. When air travel began to be more practical, purely on time-saving grounds, members of the royal family would travel out to their destination and join *Britannia* in a convenient harbour nearby to use her as their local floating home. It has meant that the British royal family have had on call their own country house abroad, with their own well-loved and well-worn possessions on board, onto which to retreat after a hard day's handshaking.

The plans to replace the old *Victoria and Albert* had been formulated before the Second World War; early drawings shown to King George VI and his Queen are essentially of the *Britannia*. But post-war austerity meant the plans were shelved until the beginning of the 1950s after a Conservative Government had been re-elected. The revised plan was for a royal yacht that would have a secondary role as a hospital ship in the event of war. This, it has been suggested, was the primary reason for building the ship but, in the only conflict in which a hospital ship was needed, in the Falklands in 1982, *Britannia* was found severely wanting. Down the years no-one had ever tried to ensure that the ship was kept up to date for her hospital role, or crucially, that her engines burned fuel compatible with the rest of the fleet. It is hard not to conclude that this

Detail left Good old-fashioned spit and polish helps buff up the shine on *Britannia*'s bell.

Below Britannia moored in the Pool of London above Tower Bridge. She exudes a special magic wherever she goes.

was because, after her launch, no-one had ever really believed in the hospital-ship role. Even the most ardent of those who have defended her cost down the years have come to accept that *Britannia* was only ever going to be just a royal yacht.

In recent years much has been made of her role as an 'ambassador' for British trade; this, too, has risen more to prominence as questions of her rising cost to the British taxpayer have become more strident, and the British monarchy at large has lost more and more support among the British public. Hard-headed businessmen the world over were never going to be swayed in their choice of British goods and services by any amount of pomp and circumstance connected with a royal yacht. In fact, signing deals on board, entertaining commercial guests during the so-called 'sea-days' have figured hardly at all in the 43 years of her time (only 63 days were spent on trade promotion between 1989–96 – nine days a year on average).

But as a royal yacht on the world stage she has performed a near-perfect coda to the story of British royal yachts. Anything that might come after is likely to be a poor imitation. She has sailed more than a

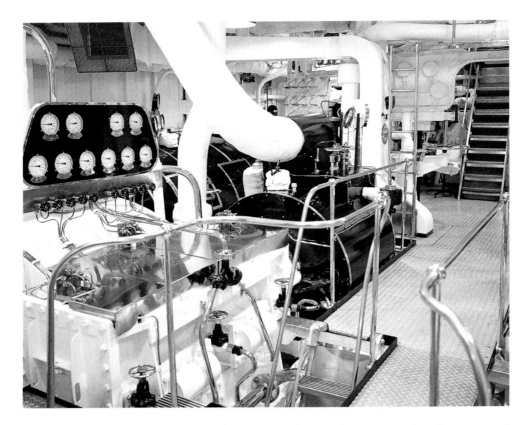

million miles on her original engines, been the venue for four royal honeymoons (although all four marriages have now ended), and the setting for countless ceremonies at which the Royal Navy excel. Nothing was more evocative of the ending of British rule over Hong Kong than the sight of the old ship slipping her moorings at midnight and sliding slowly away, her departure the final curtain of the old British Empire, just a month or so after the centenary of Queen Victoria's Diamond Jubilee at the apogee of imperial progress.

When the Admiralty asked for bids to build her, seven shipbuilding companies put in tenders. John Brown's on the Clyde signed the contract just 24 hours before King George VI died in 1952. John Brown had built both the *Queen Elizabeth* and *Queen Mary*, the largest passenger liners ever, and they would go on to build the *QEII*.

Britannia was launched on 16th April 1953 by the Queen, two months before her Coronation. The name had been kept secret. The Queen's choice, it seems, was a happy combination of the name's long pedigree in the Royal Navy, its association with her grandfather's old yacht, and its having been the name for the shore-based college, the Royal Naval College at Dartmouth, where she first met her husband.

The ship that backed down the slipways into the Clyde on that wet and windy day was the last in the Royal Navy on which the men slept in hammocks (although that no longer applies). Her crew of 21 officers and 256 'yachtsmen' (not ratings) and a Royal Marine band of 26, ran a vessel of 412 feet, with a beam of 55 feet and a draught of just over 15-and-a-half feet. Her gross tonnage is 5,862 and she can maintain a continuous speed of 21 knots. She has a range of 2,000 miles. Like all her

Above left and right Even the engine rooms are kept in pristine condition against the possibility that a royal will pop through.

Right Two of the world's most unmistakable profiles: *Britannia* and the *QEII*.

Right inset Stern stuff: the royal stamp on *Britannia's* transom.

predecessors, she has three masts and, like them, at the heel of each is a coin. The Queen had decided that her hull would be painted a distinctive royal blue rather than the traditional black. *Britannia* also has a single line in gold leaf painted right around the hull, another novelty thought up by Queen Elizabeth.

The royal apartments are all aft of the funnel, lying behind solid steel doors that separate the ship end from the yacht end. The furnishings, which have been only slightly modified down the years, represent the British royal family's preference for country-house-style living. Many of the fixtures and fittings have been handed down from earlier yachts. When the ship was being made ready in 1953, sheets and blankets from the old royal yacht were pressed into use, including those for the Queen. In the large drawing room there is a mahogany bookcase and sideboard from the last *Victoria and Albert*; the three coins left under that ship's masts are now in the bookcase. On one of the walls is a small tattered piece of silk, part of the flag flown from the sledge of the ill-fated polar explorer Captain Scott.

Some of the furniture in this room is old, some a donation from the Swedish royal family. The drawing room has a number of chintz-covered sofas and armchairs. On the floor is a silver-grey carpet running the entire length of the deck. Part of it is covered by two large Persian rugs, gifts from the Gulf states visited by the yacht with the Queen on board in 1979. There is a fireplace in the room which was intended to house a real fire, but a Royal Naval regulation which states any open fire must have a rating next to it with a fire bucket at the ready put paid to the whole idea. The fireplace is filled with a forlorn electric fire instead.

The decor is constant throughout: white painted walls and ceilings, lustre bronze metalwork and dark mahogany woodwork. Loose covers for furniture mean that changes can be made: the royals favour a green-and-white pattern; alternates include blue-and-white with a peacock motif, or a very pale cream, used when the ship is in the tropics. The

Above left The royal drawing room.

Above The royal dining room.

Inset left In 1994 *Britannia* was used for the first state visit of a British sovereign to Russia. President Boris Yeltsin and his wife were entertained on board at the end of the visit in St Petersburg.

drawing room also contains a large number of items collected from all over the world, most of them gifts from countries the ship has visited.

The dining room, which can seat 32, has chairs (all Hepplewhite style) from the old royal yacht, along with two nineteenth-century sideboards after Chippendale. In the centre of the table is the single most valuable item on the ship. It is an extraordinary solid-gold sculpture of two camels under two palm trees – a gift from the ruler of Dubai – probably worth over £1 million. It's not an especially pretty sight, but does lend itself to a good deal of speculative conversation over lunches and dinners.

Between the drawing room and the dining room, which are the two main arenas for state occasions, is the foyer and staircase which leads to the bedroom suites of the Queen and Prince Philip above on the shelter deck. Either side of the staircase on port and starboard sides are two small sitting rooms for use by the Queen (starboard) and the Prince (port). The Queen uses her sitting room more as an office when she is on board. Below the state apartments, on the main deck, are 16 cabins, each with en-suite bathrooms. Cabin 14 is a favourite as it has gold furnishings – both the Prince of Wales and Prince Edward have used this

cabin many times. The
Princess Royal and the Duke
of York prefer cabin 9, with its
muted green colour scheme.
Cabin 9, joined with cabin 11,
make up a guest suite, when
needed. Cabin 11, on its own,
has been used as a nursery.

The other side of the yacht,
forward of the funnel, is where
304 men have to live together
to run the ship. Until 1995
Britannia always had an
admiral as her commander (her
last captain was Commodore
Anthony Morrow). As a ship
of the Royal Navy she is
an independent command
answering to no-one. The reason for having an admiral in charge was
the same as it was in the nineteenth century, providing the requisite
clout needed to get things done in foreign ports when dealing with
officialdom. The change in her final command was as redolent as
anything of the end of the old ship's career.

Most of the old royal yacht rules apply to crew. For instance, there is
only a transfer out of the yacht if a member of the crew has to be
punished. They still wear soft shoes, and no orders are shouted – the
whole operation is run using hand signals to preserve peace and quiet. If
a crew member comes across royalty he merely stands still until they
have passed, saluting having been dropped as too intrusive.

The hammocks for the ratings were finally abolished in 1970. Many
were sorry to see them go, declaring they were the most comfortable
way to sleep at sea. One sailor, Leading Seaman Jamie Stewart,
complained so much that he was allowed to keep his hammock,
becoming the last man in the Navy to sleep in one.

There is little space for all the crew – or even the officers, who have
slightly more room. Apart from the kudos of being a 'yottie' on
Britannia, the men get no extra allowances and, exactly as in the past,
promotion only comes from men leaving the yacht, usually through
retirement. All the traditions as to conduct and dress apply as well,
including an insistence that all the men wear a collar and tie when they
go ashore, wherever they are in the world. Smoking is allowed below
decks but not on the upper during working hours when a standard is
flying, either at sea or in harbour. If any member of the royal family is
aboard, all the work that has to be done aft has to be completed by 9am.
If anyone has to go into the royal section after this time they have to use
the route below deck. *Britannia*, with a royal party on board, is like two
completely separate ships.

Inset above Britannia arrives in port.
Everything possible will have been
done to ensure that, once alongside,
nothing can damage her royal blue
paintwork.

Above Britannia in company with
a Royal Navy guardship, a feature
of royal yacht operations since
early times.

Right One of *Britannia's* barges –
crew as ever at the alert.

Far right Royal Marines on board
provide the necessary security in port.

Above Britannia, like her predecessors, has been a regular attender at Cowes Week, always held in the first week of August.

Below Britannia is often a focal point for the yacht racing during Cowes Week, providing a splendid marker and a reminder of more elegant days.

The Royal Marines who are aboard live in their own mess, called the barracks. They carry out the security duties, and act as sentries when required. The rest of the time they work alongside the rest of the crew, doing watches, loading stores, moving gear on deck or below. A marine band is on board whenever there's a major royal tour. One of their specialities is 'beating retreat'. When the Queen visited California in the 1980s she gave a dinner party for President Reagan and his wife. After they'd watched this ceremony, at the end of the evening Reagan is said to have remarked that, while Hollywood was the entertainment capital of the world, it could not have staged anything as theatrical. The band forms into smaller groups to play at receptions or dinner parties. The rule is for light middle-of-the-road music to be played, never pop and certainly never classical. Unusually, the band is also allowed to book itself out for private engagements, and band members can keep any money they make.

One advantage all the crew have enjoyed has been the places visited. There have been few parts of the world to which *Britannia* has not sailed. It started in 1954 with a voyage to Libya, then still a monarchy, with the Queen, Prince Philip, and both Charles and Anne on board. The following year Princess Margaret went to the West Indies, Prince Philip to the Mediterranean, and the whole family to Wales, the Isle of Man and Scotland. The Western Isles summer cruise was established early on as a part of the royal year. In August the Queen and her closest family voyage around the remoter islands of the Inner and Outer Hebrides, anchoring offshore close by a favourite picnic spot. Here, they have a barbecue alone, the only security a lone protection officer in

the distance. It is in this setting that the Queen has said she can truly relax, away from the spotlight of publicity and with her husband and children with her.

In 1956-7 Prince Philip travelled on a world tour on her, and in 1961 the Queen and the Prince went on an extended tour of West Africa. So it has gone on and on, with various members of the royal family using the yacht for official and informal visits. But there has been a decline in use over the past decade – in 1996 the Queen only used the ship for the 11 days of her summer cruise.

The most famous voyages have probably been the four honeymoons. It started in 1960 when Princess Margaret married Anthony Armstrong-Jones, later Lord Snowdon. They stepped aboard at the Tower of London for a 6,000-mile voyage to the West Indies. Instructions were given to the crew that the couple were to be left alone at all times. Princess Margaret is known to be a stickler for protocol so there was absolutely no mingling with the officers and crew at any time. All meals were taken in the state dining room, both the Princess and her husband dressing formally, she in tiara and full-length gown. The couple spent their evenings listening to Frank Sinatra and Nat King Cole records.

Thirteen years later it was the turn of Princess Anne and Captain Mark Phillips, who also spent their honeymoon in the West Indies. Earlier criticism of the use of the royal yacht for private cruises such as this was allayed in their case as the ship was en route for New Zealand and a state visit. The couple flew to Barbados to join the yacht. In their case the weather, like their marriage, was stormy with

Below Britannia was used by Princess Margaret and Anthony Armstrong-Jones (*inset*) for their honeymoon – the first of four such royal occasions, and the reason she became known as the 'love boat' by her crew.

large waves battering the ship. Both Anne and Mark were severely seasick. Princess Anne (now the Princess Royal) was much more down to earth than her aunt, as she has demonstrated since, and the crew felt able to play a number of practical jokes on her and her husband during the honeymoon.

Probably the most famous honeymoon was that of the Prince and Princess of Wales. They went to the Mediterranean in 1981 for a 16-day cruise. Aside from one formal occasion, when the President of Egypt, Anwar Sadat, and his wife came to dinner, the voyage was very informal. The Princess spent a lot of time sunbathing in her bikini. She was only 20 and very new to the whole extraordinary world of the royal family. She liked to explore the whole ship, including the crew's quarters. This was in marked contrast to Charles who only visited the 'front' of *Britannia* when invited to do so by the officers in their wardroom.

The last honeymoon on board was that of the Duke and Duchess of York who went to the Azores in 1986. The arrangements with Portuguese naval vessels to keep prying boats and planes away meant that the couple were able to enjoy almost complete privacy, picnicking ashore, fishing and diving.

There could not have been a greater contrast to all these quietly organised and intensely private affairs than the one time in her career that *Britannia* came close to fulfilling her alternate role as a hospital ship. In 1986, while she was steaming from Britain to Australia to get ready for a state visit by the Queen to the Pacific Islands, civil war broke out in the former British colony of Aden at the southern tip of the Arabian peninsula. It was known that a large number of evacuees were gathering on the beach near the town waiting for rescue. Other Royal Naval ships in the vicinity were alerted, but it was *Britannia* that was much the closest.

When the royal yacht arrived off the port it was clear a lot of fighting was taking place. Any chance she might have had to steam into the harbour and pick up the refugees was dashed when the officers on the bridge realised a full-scale battle was going on between gunboats in the

Above left and inset The 1981 honeymoon cruise of the Prince and Princess of Wales. Only a year after the couple eventually divorced in 1996, the Princess was killed in a car crash in Paris.

Right Three views during her 'Indian summer'. By the 1990s *Britannia* was aging and her future was growing increasingly uncertain. Her moment of true triumph, off Aden in 1986, had meant she could retire gracefully, having fulfilled both her original roles, as a royal yacht and a hospital ship.

harbour and tanks on shore. An added complication was the status of the ship and the rescue, and whether she would be a target herself. There were protracted negotiations with people ashore and, eventually, *Britannia* anchored off the beach near to the port where most refugees had gathered, all her floodlights on and flying three white ensigns at her mastheads.

Although the crew had been told to take only British refugees it became clear they would be taking anyone who needed help. Boats were sent ashore with officers and crew to help organise the rescue. On the first night alone they picked up 152 people from 26 countries. In all, 431 people were taken aboard *Britannia* in the first phase of the evacuation, most of them in a second state of shock at realising who their rescuer was. From the efforts off Aden *Britannia* moved down the coast and effected a further rescue of 209 people from a beach, transferring them to *HMS Jupiter* which had by then arrived to help. More rescues followed, with *Britannia* now having a Soviet liaison officer aboard to help co-ordinate the overall rescue effort in conjunction with Soviet ships in the vicinity.

Just as the ship was finally leaving she had a call from the shore that there was one person left. They turned *Britannia* around and picked up a London bus driver who had been staying in Aden for a holiday.

In all, *Britannia* rescued 1,068 people of 55 nationalities. The Queen had sent orders that the whole ship, including the state apartments, was to be made available to the rescued. After they had all left there was found to be very little damage of any kind. For the officers and crew this was their finest hour. The ship had proved herself to the rest of the Navy at last, and had done it with style.

Is she the last of a long line? Only time will tell. In the autumn of 1997, as she makes her last summer cruise, there are plans afoot to replace her with a privately financed multi-purpose ship.

The actual fate of *Britannia* herself is in the balance, too. No longer to be the British royal yacht, some want her to be turned into a tourist attraction, possibly in London's Docklands, or further up the Thames near the Tower of London perhaps. There has been a suggestion she might be bought by a British business consortium and used permanently as a floating exhibition centre sailing the world promoting Britain. Whatever happens a line will be drawn under her: the last large-scale fully dedicated royal yacht in British history.

Above Britannia leaves Portsmouth for her last voyage, to the Mediterranean, Arabian Gulf, Indian Ocean and the Far East, for the handover of Hong Kong in 1997.

Above The sun has set on the last significant part of the old British Empire, and *Britannia* sails off with the last Governor of Hong Kong on board. In many ways *Britannia* has been a left-over, like Hong Kong, from earlier, more sedate and more certain days.

Right Prince Charles and ex-Governor Chris Patten aboard *Britannia* after the ceremonies marking the handover of Hong Kong to the Chinese in June 1997.

EPILOGUE

By the late 1990s, across the world, royal yachts were getting rarer. And there were fewer royal families than before the wars to own them. Presidential yachts, despite the predominance of republics, were also on the wane: too slow, too expensive. In many ways those left were anachronisms, leftovers from more sedate, more elegant times. The ostentation displayed in any number of the yachts owned by royal families in the Middle East or parts further east, was more than counterbalanced by those remaining European royal families who maintained a royal yacht with the emphasis on quiet dignity. While the quasi-feudal systems in the Gulf states or Brunei meant their rulers could continue to do more or less as they pleased, the question of the cost of maintaining royal yachts was a growing and more urgent one in Europe.

The argument, used a good deal in Britain – that a royal yacht lent weight to the importance and self-esteem of the whole nation merely by displaying itself – seemed at best archaic, at worst yet more self-delusion. If the United States did not need symbols like these, why should Britain – no longer a maritime nation of any significance? Royal yachts increasingly appeared to belong to that earlier time when the royal family was an immutable part of a seamless tradition, locked into history, and when the certainty, which royal yachts represented in the solidity of their form, was unquestioned. The cost, although it was counted, was thought to be well worth the return. By the mid 1990s cost was, above all else, what had to count.

Royal yachts have always brought a magic of their own to the trappings of state. That they are different from state yachts is demonstrable, for unlike, say, the presidential yachts of the United States, royal yachts remain in the family as a private place to which their owners can retreat, and fill with their own belongings, permanently placed. In a world that is generally determined to call to account every cost borne by the taxpayer, the discrepancy between an ostensibly public ownership of a royal yacht through state funding, and its private use by the monarch, is one which now has to be squared.

As the role of monarchies in the modern world has come increasingly

Right Final tour of duty: *Britannia* in Hong Kong. Royal yachts were getting much rarer by the 1990s, as were yachts or ships used by republics. Only in the Gulf states has there been no sign of a desire to reduce the building and running costs of these elegant but pricey vessels.

under scrutiny, so all these hitherto private issues have come out into the open. These matters hardly touch monarchs living outside Europe, even including Japan, which remains a traditional culture despite its modern economic successes. The Scandinavians solved the problem years ago when they decided heavily to downplay the rituals (and therefore expense) of monarchy, and to go instead for a low-key approach. This is mirrored, to some extent, in Holland and Belgium, and even Spain. The question of royal yachts in each of these countries in the future is likely to be resolved by their fully private ownership – a method increasingly employed by the bulk of royals in the rest of the world.

In Britain, such a course would still seem to be problematic. If, as seemed likely when this book went to press, late in 1997, *Britannia* was not going to get a hugely expensive refit, then it was still most likely that her replacement, probably of the same size and costing around £65 million, would be funded from the public purse. The argument for doing this, assiduously canvassed by monarchists, was that there would be a great benefit in using such a vessel to promote trade. It was all a long way from the reasons why royalty came to use royal yachts in the past. If the underlying purpose of a royal (or state) yacht was – and is – to help to trumpet the difference between royal personages and the rest, nothing would be more calculated to do the opposite than what the proposers suggested. Those pushing it hardest did not appear to recognise the logical absurdity, if royal mystique is to be preserved, of jamming royalty up against their subjects.

The least likely option appeared to be that the British royal family would fund any future yacht out of their own purse, and the idea of a smaller successor being built with reduced running costs had hardly been mentioned.

Left The Queen makes history as she boards a New Zealand Airlines commercial jet for her visit.

Above One proposal for a replacement for *Britannia* has her as a hybrid sail-training ship, a platform for selling British goods, and a conference centre. The royals would have use of the section aft.

As it happens, by 1997, the Queen had already travelled by commercial jet from Britain to New Zealand, roped off with her entourage in the first-class section. It was as potent a sign as any that things were changing, and might have to change a lot more. So, one completely different and seemingly solid proposal, put forward by a consortium of retired admirals, yachtsmen and businessmen, for a royal sail-training ship, did not get the scorn poured over it that a few years before it would have merited.

The concept was for a 370-foot long, 48-foot beam, three-masted square-rigged, multi-engined ship (see drawing), with a crew of 60. There would a capacity for 180 trainees, for this vessel has been conceived as a multi-purpose ship, combining the functions of royal yacht, training ship and trade promoter, through exhibitions that could be held on board. She would be powered by diesel-electric engines, giving her a range of around 6,000 miles under power, an economical speed of 15 knots and a top speed of 20 knots. She would be built to conform with all the new environmental and other standards with a strong emphasis on energy efficiency. Apart from the royal apartments, she would have two theatres, one of 144 seats, the other of 36, for conferences, and plenty of exhibition space, too.

In a neat twist, the consortium suggested that the royal apartments, aft of the mainmast, would actually be bigger than those on *Britannia*. At her stern there would be a retractable helipad, she would have a garage for two cars, and space for seven boats, including a royal barge.

Her crew would be drawn from the merchant navy and from sail-training establishments, although she would still have a naval officer as

her commander. The cadets carried by this ship would be from youth, commercial and government organisations, and from the armed services. Their purpose, apart from helping to run the ship, would also be to act as young 'ambassadors' when she was on state, diplomatic or trade missions.

The cost of this ship was put at about £65 million, half of which had apparently already been pledged. Once built, the plan would be for the ship to be self-financing from fees paid by the royal family for her use, from the government for its use, and through charging trainees for the time they were aboard. There was the possibility that the ship could be opened to the public from time to time, generating more income.

Above Sailors line the deck of the carrier *HMS Illustrious* as *Britannia*, carrying the Prince of Wales and Chris Patten, takes part in a ceremonial 'steam past' after the handover of Hong Kong. The future of *Illustrious* is uncertain as well.

Right The Queen and Commodore Anthony Morrow, having bid farewell to the families of *Britannia*'s crew on the final summer cruise, 1997.

If this ship is ever to be built, the main plus point from the British Government's side is her independence from public funds, although history suggests government money would end up topping up any shortfalls. But huge problems remain. One, unclear in the autumn of 1997, was the attitude of the Queen to this proposal. Known to be very unhappy at any suggestion that *Britannia* be turned into a tourist attraction anywhere, sold off to anyone or, indeed, used in any way after decommissioning as a royal yacht, she might be thought to be less than happy over this proposal which tries, in beating off the crucial question of costs, to be all things to all men – and women.

As this book has shown there is no logic as such in building *royal* yachts, unless it be the logic which insists monarchies are themselves both logical and right. While this might have been axiomatic a hundred years ago when, as it happened, the British could well afford to lavish money on their Queen and, indeed, believed it proper that they should, today the calculations increasingly swing around the twin questions of cost-effectiveness and the future of the monarchy.

For the rest of the world, some royal and a few official state yachts may remain. This is a field on which only the very rich or reckless can now play. The new yacht for the Sultan of Brunei, shortly to be launched, was designed to be bigger than the biggest that the King of Saudi Arabia currently has in his fleet. If this sounds familiar, it is. If the arena for this regal rivalry has shifted East, never to return, then it reflects the age-old vanity of monarchs.

Royal yachts have had their heyday; in truth they belong to a past where everyone not only knew their place, but was, by and large, ignorant of any possible alternative to it.

There was one positive aspect. The great Victorian age produced a wealth of beauty in its royal yachts we may never be able to match again – that happy affinity of design with practicality – nor would we think it sensible. We may yet marvel at Versailles while being aware of the system which produced it, just as we can look at images of the great steam yachts, and still be aware of the awful conditions suffered by both builders and those who did the real work on board.

The true tragedy lies in a more prosaic fact: none of the beautifully crafted and lovingly maintained Victorian steam yachts remains in its original form for us to gaze upon; in that alone is the greatest loss of all.

LIST OF ALL KNOWN
ROYAL AND STATE YACHTS

NAME OF VESSEL	LAUNCH YEAR	OVERALL LENGTH (ft)	BEAM (ft)	DRAUGHT (ft)	APPROX. TONNAGE	NOTES
EUROPE						
GREAT BRITAIN						
Mary	1660	52	19	8	100	The world's first royal yacht
Royal Escape	—	30	15	7	34	
Anne	1661	52	19	7	100	
Bezan	1661	34	14	7	35	
Katherine (1)	1661	49	19	7	94	
Minion	—	28	12	5	22	
Charles (1)	1662	36	14	7	38	
Jemmy	1662	31	13	6	25	
Henrietta	1663	52	19	7	104	
Merlin	1666	53	20	6	109	
Monmouth	1666	52	20	8	103	
Navy	1666	48	18	8	74	
Saudadoes	1670	50	18	8	86	
Cleveland	1671	53	21	8	107	
Queenborough	1671	30	13	7	29	
Deale	1673	32	13	6	28	
Isle of Wight	1673	33	13	6	30	
Kitchen	1674	52	20	9	103	
Katherine (2)	1674	36	21	9	135	
Portsmouth (1)	1674	57	21	7	133	
Charles (2)	1675	54	21	8	120	
Charlot	1677	62	21	9	142	
Mary (2)	1677	67	22	9	166	
Henrietta (2)	1679	65	22	8	162	
Izabella Bezan	1680	46	16	—	52	
Fubbs	1682	63	21	10	148	Named for the Duchess of Portsmouth
Isabella (1)	1683	60	19	12	114	
William & Mary (1)	1694	61	22	10	152	
Squirrel	1694	36	—	—	37	
Scout	1695	14	—	—	38	
Queenborough (2)	1701	—	—	—	44	
Soesdyke	1702	58	20	9	106	
Portsmouth (2)	1702	43	17	9	66	Renamed Medina
Isabella (2)	1703	—	—	—	104	

Name of Vessel	Launch Year	Overall Length (ft)	Beam (ft)	Draught (ft)	Approx. Tonnage	Notes
Drake	1705	—	—	—	50	
Dublin	1709	60	—	—	148	
Bolton	1709	38	15	8	42	
Charlot (2)	1710	58	23	10	155	
Carolina	1710	71	—	—	177	Originally *Peregrine*; renamed *Royal Caroline*, 1733
Chatham (1)	1710	44	—	—	60	
Chatham (2)	1741	47	17	8	74	
Portsmouth (3)	1742	48	18	9	83	
Royal Caroline	1749	72	25	11	232	Renamed *Royal Charlotte*, 1761
Dorset	1753	65	22	11	164	
Plymouth	1755	53	18	10	88	
Augusta	1771	65	23	11	184	Renamed *Princess Augusta*, 1773
Portsmouth (4)	1794	70	19	12	102	
Plymouth (2)	1796	53	19	10	96	
Royal Sovereign	1804	80	26	11	278	
William & Mary (2)	1807	70	23	11	199	
Royal George	1817	103	26.5	11.5	330	Finally broken up in 1905
Prince Regent	1820	96	25.5	11.5	—	
Royal Charlotte (2)	1824	75.5	23	8	202	
Royal Adelaide	1833	50	—	—	50	Miniature frigate; broken up 1877
Victoria & Albert (1)	1842	225	33	14	1034	Renamed *Osborne*, 1855
Fairy	1844	161	21	7	317	Screw-propelled iron yacht
Elfin	1848	112	13	5	98	Taken to pieces, 1901
Victoria & Albert II	1854	300	40	16	2470	Broken up and burnt, 1904
Alberta	1863	160	23	8	370	Broken up, 1913
Osborne (2)	1870	250	36	15	1850	Sold, 1908
Victoria & Albert (3)	1899	380	50	21	5500	Broken up, 1955
Alexandra	1908	275	40	13	2050	Sold, 1925 to Norway as *Prince Olaf*
Britannia	1953	412	55	16	5862	Due for decommissioning, 1997
GERMANY						
Alexandria	—	92	—	—	99 TM	
Grille (1)	1858	185	24	9	—	Used in the Baltic
Kaiseradler	1875	268	34	14	—	
Lorelei	—	90	—	—	—	Possibly the first *Hohenzollern*
Hohenzollern (2)	1893	383	46	23	3773 TM	
Hohenzollern (3)	1913	520	62	19	7300 DISP	Never completed
Grille (2)	1934	377	44	11	2560 DISP	Sold after the war; scrapped, 1949
Osterland I	—	180	23	7	—	Both converted from coastal
Osterland II	—	180	23	7	—	minesweepers; East German; fate unknown
FRANCE						
L'Aigle	1858	160	25	10	—	
Jérôme Napoléon	1859	230	24	12	—	
La Reine Hortense	1867	230	24	12	—	All estimates
Thistle	—	—	—	—	—	Used by Empress Eugénie after her exile

ROYAL YACHTS OF THE WORLD

NAME OF VESSEL	LAUNCH YEAR	OVERALL LENGTH (ft)	BEAM (ft)	DRAUGHT (ft)	APPROX. TONNAGE	NOTES
HOLLAND						
De Leeuw	1826	120	18	6	—	World's first royal steam yacht
De Valk	1864	250	31	12	1042 TM	
Piet Hein	1937	102	19	5	151 TM	
DENMARK						
Elephanten	1687	92	23	9	—	
Cronen	—	—	—	—	—	
Slesvig	1845	176	26	8	740 DISP	
Falkin	—	—	—	—	—	
Dannebrog (1)	1879	199	27	10	650 TM	
Dannebrog (2)	1931	207	34	12	1070 TM	Still sailing
SWEDEN						
Amphion	1778	160	—	—	—	Known to be shallow draught
Drott	1877	175	27	12	630 TM	
NORWAY						
Norge	1947	263	38	14.5	1611	Ex-*Philante*, Sir Thomas Sopwith's yacht
BELGIUM						
Alberta	1896	257	34	15	1322	GL Watson design; ex-*Margerita*
Avila	—	—	—	—	—	
ITALY						
Savoia I	1883	305	41	—	3266 DISP	
Trinacria	1883	463	51	—	9199 DISP	Ex-*America*
Savoia II	1922	390	49	15	4388 TM	
Iela	—	—	—	—	—	2 yachts of this name; no details
PAPAL STATE						
Immacolata Concezione	1859	178	27	16	627	British built; use unknown
SPAIN						
Giralda	1894	306	35	18	1506 TM	
Azor	1949	153	25	11	—	Formerly Franco's yacht
PORTUGAL						
Safo	—	—	—	—	—	
Amelia	—	—	—	—	147	Owned by King Carlos, 19th century
Amelia II	1880	148	21	11	301TM	Ex-*Fair Geraldine*
Amelia III	1900	220	30	11	899TM	Ex-*Banshee*
GREECE						
Amphitrite	1867	—	—	—	—	
Salamis	1928	—	—	—	2020	
Bouboulina	—	—	—	—	1950	
Polemistes	—	—	—	—	—	Ex-*Algerine* type minesweeper
Theseus	1963	—	—	—	—	
Argo	1943	325	—	—	—	Former Onassis yacht; originally built as Canadian frigate

NAME OF VESSEL	LAUNCH YEAR	OVERALL LENGTH (ft)	BEAM (ft)	DRAUGHT (ft)	APPROX. TONNAGE	NOTES
YUGOSLAVIA						
Krajina	1928	164	26	4	250	Used on the Danube
Dubrovnik	1931	—	—	—	—	British-built destroyer
Jabranka	1939	213	26	10	567	
Galeb	1939	385	51	18	5182 DISP	
Kozara	—	—	—	—	—	
Podgorna	—	130	—	—	—	For sale, 1997
Istranka	1959	150	25	9	—	
MONACO						
Hirondelle	—	—	—	—	200	
Princess Alice	1891	180	27	12	593 TM	
Hirondelle II	—	—	—	—	—	
Deo Juvante	—	133	—	—	80	Also *Deo Juvante II*
Stalca	—	—	—	—	80	Also *Stalca II*; *Carostefal*
Pacha III	1936	119	18	8	—	Owned by Princess Caroline
ROMANIA						
Luceafarul	1930	300	36	15	1574 TM	Ex-*Nahlin*
BULGARIA						
Nadiejda	1898	200	23	13	715 GROSS	
RUSSIA						
Standart (1)	1703	190	23	8		Peter the Great's original flagship
Queen Victoria	1846	95	22	12	—	
Standart (2)	—	—	—	—	—	Early 19th century
Livadia	1880	235	153	18	11802 TM	'Admiral Popov' style circular ship
Polar Star	1888	337	46	15	3270 TM	
Standart (3)	—	—	—	—	1100	Built in Bordeaux, mid 19th century
Standart	1895	450	50	20	4334 TM	Ended as Soviet ship *Marti*
AUSTRO-HUNGARY						
Greif	—	—	—	—	—	
Fantasie	1857	176	16	9	330 TM	
Miramar	1872	269	33	14	1830 TM	
Ul	1911	187	29	16	709 TM	Sold and renamed *Sayonara*

THE AMERICAS
USA

NAME OF VESSEL	LAUNCH YEAR	OVERALL LENGTH (ft)	BEAM (ft)	DRAUGHT (ft)	APPROX. TONNAGE	NOTES
River Queen	—	—	—	—	556	Used by President Lincoln
Despatch	1873	174	26	12	560	
Sylph	—	123	20	—	152	
Dolphin	1884	240	32	14	1465	
Mayflower	1897	275	36	17	1779 GROSS	Ended as refugee ship *Mala*
Sequoia	1925	99	19	4	110	
Williamsburg	1930	244	36	16	1920 DISP	Former coastguard cutter
Potomac	1934	370	24	8	370	Still in use as pleasure craft
Leonore	—	92	17	—	—	Both renamed by successive presidents (ie, *Honey Fitz*)
Margie	—	64	15	—	—	

Name of Vessel	Launch Year	Overall Length (ft)	Beam (ft)	Draught (ft)	Approx. Tonnage	Notes
MEXICO						
Sotavento	1947	166	28	10	—	
Chito	—	—	—	—	—	
DOMINICAN REPUBLIC						
Mella	—	—	—	—	—	
HAITI						
Ferrier	1898	264	34	14	851 GROSS	Presidential yacht, 1913-15
VENEZUELA						
10 de Dicembre	—	—	—	—	—	
ARGENTINA						
Presidente Sarmiento	—	—	—	—	—	
Tequara	—	—	—	—	—	
THE MIDDLE EAST						
MOROCCO						
Marrakesh	—	—	—	—	—	
Oued Daheb	—	—	—	—	—	
LIBYA						
Hannibal	1975	131	26	7	—	
EGYPT						
Sayed Pasha	1847	156	17	2.5	—	
Said	1858	250	28	—	900	
Faid Gihaad	1858	383	—	—	—	
Mahroussa	1866	478	43	18	3762 GROSS	Figures are for final rebuild
Cleopatra	—	—	—	—	—	
Safa El-Bahr	1894	200	27	12	—	
Khassed Kheir	1928	238	32	3.5	—	
TURKEY						
Vassitei Tudjaret	1847	210	52	20	—	
Taliah	1864	—	—	—	—	
Teslifiyeh	1898	—	—	—	—	
Erthrogroul	1903	264	28	14	—	
Savarona	1931	440	52	20	6000+	Built for American owner first
IRAQ						
Faisal I	1923	203	30	13	—	Originally the *Restless*
Qadissaya Saddam	1987	269	43	12	—	Apparently sold to Saudi Arabia
Zinat al Bihaar	—	—	—	—	—	
SAUDI ARABIA						
King Abdul Said	—	—	—	—	—	
Al Salamah	1973	380	—	—	—	
Al Riyadh	1978	212	32	10	—	
Abdul Aziz	1984	482	60	16	—	Still world's largest royal yacht
Al Yamamah	1987	269	43	12	—	Formerly *Qadissaya Saddam*
Lady Moura	1991	344	61	16	—	

Name of Vessel	Launch Year	Overall Length (ft)	Beam (ft)	Draught (ft)	Approx. Tonnage	Notes
Bahrain						
Pearl Star	1980	155	27	7	—	
Awal II	1990	214	30	12	—	
Jameel	—	—	—	—	—	
Qatar						
Al Menwar	1987	207	32	8	—	
Fath al Kheir	1978	152	22	13	—	
Al Jubail	—	—	—	—	—	
Abu Dhabi						
Azzam	1987	177	30	8	—	
Dhafit	—	—	—	—	—	
Oman						
Fulk al-Salomah	—	—	—	—	—	
Al Said	1982	341	53	16	—	
Zinat al Bhaar	1988	173	30	12	—	
Persia/Iran						
Shahsavar	1936	173	25	11	—	Used in Caspian Sea
Kish	1970	122	25	7	—	Used in Persian Gulf
AFRICA						
Nigeria						
Hoffman River	—	—	—	—	—	
Ogina B	—	—	—	—	—	
Liberia						
President Edward						
James Reye	—	—	—	—	—	
Zaire						
Kamanyola	—	—	—	—	—	
Zanzibar						
HMS Glasgow	1878	210	29	16	1416 DISP	Present from Queen Victoria to the Sultan
Seyyid Khalifa	—	—	—	—	—	
ASIA						
Burma						
Tsekya Yeen Byan	1871	200	26	18	—	Means 'flying scud'
Siam/Thailand						
Vesatri	—	144	22	11	280	
Maha Chakri	—	—	—	—	—	Visited England in 1897
Chantara	1961	230	35	10	870 DISP	
Japan						
The Emperor	1857	—	—	—	300	
Hiyodori	1966	197	23	8	445 DISP	
Matsunami	1995	115	26	11	165 DISP	

ROYAL YACHTS OF THE WORLD

Name of Vessel	Launch Year	Overall Length (ft)	Beam (ft)	Draught (ft)	Approx. Tonnage	Notes
PHILIPPINES						
Banahaw	1908	287	33	16	1227 GROSS	Inter-war state yacht
Apo	—	184	33	10	850 DISP	Formerly US Navy minesweeper
Ang Pangulo	1958	258	43	21	2239	Built as part of Japanese war reparations
MALAYSIA						
Bonita	—	—	—	—	—	
Puten Kayangam	—	—	—	—	—	
Puteri Sabah II	—	—	—	—	—	
BRUNEI						
Khalifah	1987	142	—	—	—	
Tits	—	180	—	—	—	
Teeth	—	—	—	—	—	
Bolkiah I	—	—	—	—	—	
TONGA						
Titilupe	—	34	—	—	—	Also used as auxiliary patrol craft

This list does not include vessels chartered as royal or state yachts or racing (sailing) yachts from the 19th century onwards.

Tonnage is measured in different ways for ships. Because I have been dealing with ships over a long period of time, and where different tonnage is given, I have been unable to be consistent in the figures given. Wherever possible I have said which tonnage measurement is being used.

Displacement tonnage: This is the total weight of the ship and everything on board; the standard way of describing the size of warships.

Gross tonnage: This is the total cubic capacity of all enclosed space at 100 cubic feet to the ton.

Tons burden or burthen: This was the old way of measuring carrying capacity based on the number of 'tuns' (barrels) of wine that could be put in the hold of a ship.

Thames Measurement (TM) tonnage: Used exclusively for yachts (including steam yachts) this was brought in by the Royal Thames Yacht Club in 1855 to provide a fairer means of handicapping yachts for races. It is based on a formula:

$$\frac{(L - B) \times B \times \frac{1}{2}B}{94}$$

Where L is the length in feet from stem to stern; B is the beam in feet.

To take an actual example in the list above, the Hohenzollern II. Her length was 383, her beam 46. This gives in the formula the following:

$$\frac{(383 - 43) \times 43 \times 21.5}{94} = 3343$$

The 40 tons discrepancy is due to the slight inaccuracy in the figures given above; TM tonnage was a very accurate measurement of a ship's exact dimensions.

BIBLIOGRAPHY

Aitchison, David: Royal Standard, Red Ensign, Pall Mall Press, London 1958

Barnett, Correlli: Engage the Enemy More Closely, Hodder and Stoughton, London, 1991

Brouwer, Norman: International Register of Historic Ships, Anthony Nelson, Oswestry, 1985

Conway's History of the Ship; various volumes, Conway Maritime, London

Crabtree, Reginald: Luxury Yachts, David and Charles, Newton Abbott, 1973

Crabtree, Reginald: Royal Yachts of Europe, David and Charles, Newton Abbott, 1976

Crone, G C E: De Jachten der Oranjes, NV Swets & Zeitlinger, Amsterdam, 1937

Drummond, Maldwin: Salt-Water Palaces, Debrett, London, 1980

Feiling, Keith: A History of England, Macmillan, London 1966

Feversham, Lord: Great Yachts, Anthony Blond, London 1970

Gavin, C M: Royal Yachts, Rich and Cowan, London, 1932

Heckstall-Smith, Anthony: Sacred Cowes, Anthony Blond, London 1965

Hoey, Brian: The Royal Yacht Britannia, Patrick Stephens Ltd, Yeovil, 1995

Hofman, Erik: The Steam Yachts, Nautical Publishing Co, Lymington, 1970

Irving, John: The King's Britannia, Seeley Service and Co, London, 1936

Jane's Fighting Ships, Jane's Publishing, London, various annual editions

Keegan, John: The Price of Admiralty, Hutchison, London, 1988

Kennedy, Paul: The Rise and Fall of British Naval Mastery, Macmillan, London 1983

McGowan, A P: Royal Yachts, NMM, London, 1953

Madge, Tim: Long Voyage Home, Simon and Schuster, London, 1993

Marshall, Chris (ed): Encyclopedia of Ships, Blitz, London, 1995

Marwick, Arthur: The Deluge, Penguin, London, 1965

Morris, James: Heaven's Command, Penguin, London, 1979

Odell, Peter: Oil and World Power, Penguin, London 1970

Phillips-Birt, Douglas: History of Yachting, Elm Tree, London 1974

Phillips-Birt, Douglas: The Cumberland Fleet, Royal Thames Yacht Club, London, 1978

Robinson, Bill: Legendary Yachts, David McKay, London, 1971

Stevenson, John: British Society, 1914-45, Penguin, London, 1984

Victoria, Queen: Leaves from the Journal of Our Life in the Highlands, Smith Elder, London, 1868

Weintraub, Stanley: Victoria, An Intimate Biography, Truman Talley, New York 1987

Yergin, Daniel: The Prize, Simon and Schuster, London, 1991

PICTURE CREDITS

AKG London: p77, p78, p116 (inset)

Beken of Cowes: p10, p17, p68, p74, p76, p82, p84, p85, p87, p88, p90, p91 (inset), p92, p96, p115, p116, p117, p118 (top), p119, p121 (top left), p122, p123, p127, p128 (bottom), p143 (top), p158, p160, (bottom), p161 (top left), p165, p168, p169, p171 (bottom), p173 (top)

Bridgeman Art Library: p27, p112/113, p121 (top right), p124, p125

British Museum: p12

Christie's Images: p38/39

Corbis Ltd: p136, p137, p139, p150, p151 (bottom), p155 (top)

ET Archive: p12, p44

Franklin D Roosevelt Library: p126, p137 (top), p139, p140, p141

Frank Spooner Pictures: p153 (top), p161 (bottom), p166

Gamma: p143 (bottom), p156 (top, middle), p174, p175 (top), p181

Getty Images (Hulton Deutsch): p84, p94 (inset), p97, p102, p108/109, p110, p120, p121, p134 (top), p138, p147 (top), p153 (top), p154 (top), p160 (top), p171 (inset)

Glasgow City Archives: p81

Harry S Truman Library: p149 (bottom left), p149 (bottom right)

Howard and Horsefield: p131

Illustrated London News: p50, p51, p53, p54, p55, p56, p57, p60, p61, p62, p63, p64, p65, p66, p67, p73, p76, p77, p78/79, p87 (inset), p89

JS Library International: p15, p16

Kos Picture Source: p169 (bottom left), p170, p171 (bottom), p173 (middle)

Roger Lean-Vercoe: p130

Malcolm Wood: p156 (bottom), p159 (middle)

Mary Evans Picture Library: p10, p13, p14, p18, p19, p20, p21, p22, p23, p24, p25, p26, p28, p30, p33 (inset), p34 (inset), p36/37, p38, p40, p41, p42, p43, p44, p45, p46, p47, p48, p49, p58, p59, p70, p71, p78, p81, p92, p93, p94, p95, p98, p99, p111, p112, p118 (bottom)

Ingram Murray: p37 (bottom)

National Maritime Museum Picture Library: p11, p29, p31, p32, p33, p34, p35, p69, p83, p91, p130, (bottom), p132, p146, p147(bottom), p148

Popperfoto: p128, p142, p144, p145, p180/181

Rex features: p150, p151 (top), p151 (inset), p152, p153 (inset), p154 (middle), p155 (middle bottom), p157, p159 (top), p161 (top right), p162, p163, p164, p165, p167 (bottom), p168 (top), p169 (bottom right), p175 (inset bottom), p178

Royal Archives: p100, p101, p102, p103, p104, p105, p106, p107, p110, p123, p125

Royal Yacht Britannia: p164 (top left), p166, p167 (top)

Shtandart Project: p37 (top)

Sipa Press: p172, p176

TRH Pictures: p133, p135, p136, p144 (bottom right)

TRM Pictures: p134 (inset)

Yachting Photographics: p127

INDEX

Portsmouth Yard
31 March 1893

Wooven

Chief Constructor

29 July 1872

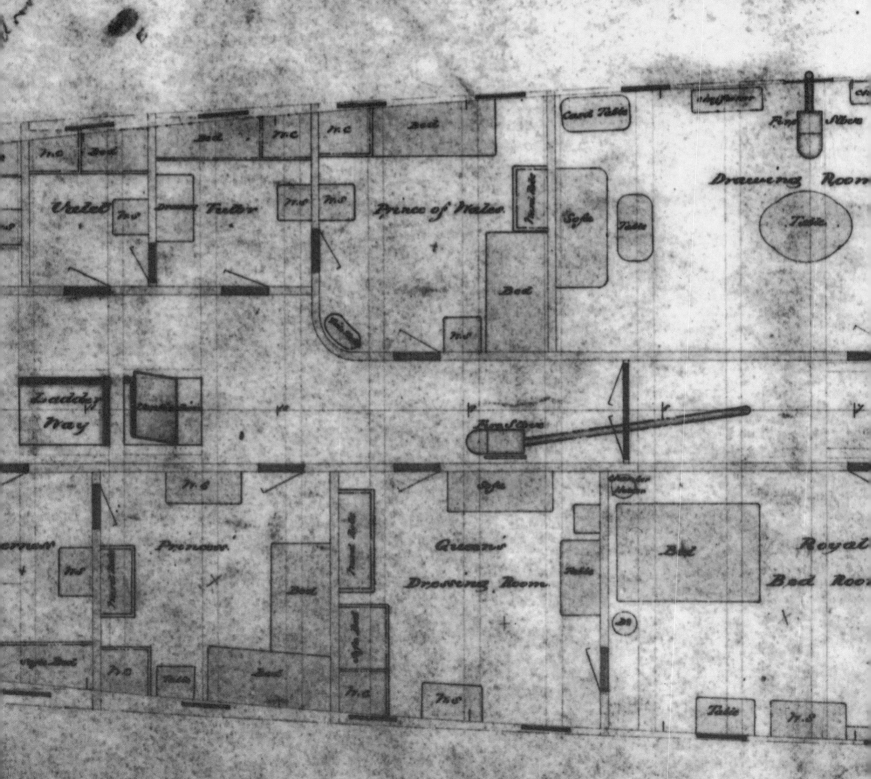